Selected Poems of René Char

René Char
                    you are a poet who believes
in the power of beauty
            to right all wrongs.
                    I believe it also.

                                        William Carlos Williams

Selected Poems of René Char

EDITED BY MARY ANN CAWS AND TINA JOLAS

A NEW DIRECTIONS BOOK

The epigraph by William Carlos Williams, from "To a Dog Injured in the Street," *The Collected Poems of William Carlos Williams*, Vol. II (Copyright © 1954 by William Carlos Williams), is reprinted by permission of New Directions Publishing Corporation.

Some of the translations in this volume were originally published in the following magazines: *Botteghe Oscure X* (Denis Devlin and Jackson Mathews), *Pequod* (Mark Hutchinson, Mark Rudman, Mary Ann Caws, and Patricia Terry), *Sulfur* (Gustaf Sobin), *Talisman* (Gustaf Sobin), *Transition Forty-eight* (Eugène Jolas), *Transition Forty-nine* (Samuel Beckett). Many other translations were previously included in the following books: *Hypnos Waking: Poems and Prose*, by René Char, edited by Jackson Mathews (Random House, 1956); *Lightning*, by Nancy Kline (Northeastern University Press, 1981); *Poems of René Char* (Princeton University Press, 1976), translated by Mary Ann Caws and Jonathan Griffin.

The poems from *Le Marteau sans maître/The Hammer with No Master* are reprinted by permission of La Librairie José Corti and those from *Les Matinaux/The Dawn Breakers* by Bloodaxe Books. The French texts of all other poems by René Char are those which appeared in *Oeuvres complètes, Aromates chasseurs, Chants de la Balandrane, Fenêtres dormantes et porte sur le toit, Les Voisinages de Van Gogh*, and *Éloge d'une Soupçonée* and are reprinted by permission of the publisher, Editions Gallimard.

Manufactured in the United States of America
New Directions Books are published on acid-free paper.
First published clothbound and as New Directions Paperbook 734 in 1992
Published simultaneously in Canada by Penguin Books Canada Limited

New Directions Books are published for James Laughlin
by New Directions Publishing Corporation,
80 Eighth Avenue, New York 10011

Continued on last page of book

Contents

THE TRANSLATORS

Paul Auster
Samuel Beckett
Mary Ann Caws
Cid Corman
Denis Devlin
Jonathan Griffin
Mark Hutchinson
Eugène Jolas
Nancy Kline
Jackson Mathews

W. S. Merwin
Christopher Prendergast
Mark Rudman
Frederick Seidel
William Jay Smith
Gustaf Sobin
Patricia Terry
William Carlos Williams
James Wright

René Char Bio-Bibliography

*c.*1836   Charlemagne, a foundling, ill-treated by the Mont Ventoux
farmers with whom he has been put out to work, flees southward
until he reaches L'Isle-sur-Sorgue, where he finds work with a
merchant of plaster. He will inherit the business, and pass it on to
his son, Émile, who shortens the name (now Char Magne) to the
simple syllable Char.

1885   Émile Char marries Julia Rouget, the daughter of a master-
mason; when she dies of tuberculosis, he marries his young sister-
in-law, Marie-Thérèse, and they have four children: Julia, Albert,
Émilienne, and René-Émile.

1907   Birth of René-Émile, June 14, at "Les Névons," L'Isle-sur-
Sorgue.

1918–   Death of Émile Char. René, after boarding at the Lycée
d' Avignon, is in Marseille at seventeen, supposed to be applying
himself to business classes; he is reading: Plutarch, Villon,
Racine, Baudelaire. He is employed with a fruit merchant in
Cavaillon.

1926   Paul Éluard publishes *Capitale de la douleur,* a book which will be
of great importance to René Char, who is in Nîmes in 1927,
doing his military service, and collaborating with local literary
reviews.

1928   *Les Cloches sur le coeur,* published in Nîmes, with Le Rouge et le
Noir, will later be disavowed, except for the poem "Le Veilleur
naïf."

1929   *Arsenal* is published with Méridien, in Nîmes, and Éluard comes
to L'Isle-sur-Sorgue; he will later introduce Char to Breton,
Crevel, and Aragon in Paris. Char joins the surrealist movement
in December, joins their battles, and publishes in *La Révolution
surréaliste.* ("Profession de foi du sujet" in no. 12.)

1930   *Ralentir travaux,* written by Breton, Char, and Éluard. With the
Éditions surréalistes–José Corti, he publishes *Artine,* a long
poem, and, in 1931, *L'Action de la justice est éteinte.*

1932   Marriage with Georgette Goldstein. He writes *Abondance viendra*
(1933).

1934	Counter-manifestations in Paris against the right wing forces; Char signs Breton's anti-fascist manifesto. *Le Marteau sans maître*, a collection of his poems since 1927, appears with Corti, prefaced by Tzara, illustrated by Kandinsky. Char drifts away from the surrealists as a group, although remaining close friends with Éluard and Crevel. He returns to L'Isle-sur-Sorgue.
1935	Tzara and his wife, the painter Greta Knutson, visit Char in L'Isle. Crevel commits suicide.
1936–1939	Char falls ill with septicemia, and recuperates over the next two years in the mountain village of Céreste, and then on the coast with Georgette, seeing Éluard and his wife Nusch frequently. Writes *Moulin premier*, his first "aphoristic verses." Éluard places it with Guy Levis Mano, a poet-printer who also publishes *Placard pour un chemin des écoliers*, dedicated to the children of Spain, and, in 1938, *Dehors la nuit est gouvernée*. The epic poem *Le Visage nuptial* is published by the Imprimerie Beresniak. Char contributes to the *Cahiers d'Art*, edited by Christan Zervos, whose wife Yvonne will become an intimate and resourceful friend.
1939	Called up, stationed on the frontier in Alsace; when the Germans invade France (May–June 1940), he fights his way down to the south of France, where he is demobilized in the summer of 1940. Returns to Georgette and L'Isle, but denounced as an anti-Fascist married to a Jew. By 1941, back in Céreste, he establishes contacts with other resistance networks, and in 1942, as "le Capitaine Alexandre," engages in sabotage missions. Officially enrolls in the Forces Françaises Combattantes and as regional head of a partisan group.
1944	After the Liberation, resumes publication of his poems in reviews: *Fontaine, Cahiers du Sud, Cahiers d'Art*.
1945	Publishes *Seuls demeurent* (Gallimard), bringing him the friendship of Braque and Camus, as well as general acclaim.
	In 1946 *Feuillets d'Hypnos*, his wartime journal, appears with Gallimard. In Nice, he meets Matisse, who will illustrate *Le Poème pulvérisé* in 1948, for the Editions Fontaine.
1947	Yvonne Zervos organizes an exhibition of painters at the Palais des Papes in Avignon, and Char writes on Braque's painting.
1948	First performance on the radio of his play *Le Soleil des eaux*, with

music by Pierre Boulez. *Fureur et mystère* appears with Gallimard, including his writing from 1938–44.

In 1949 publishes *Le Soleil des eaux,* illustrated by Braque, with another play: *Claire* (Gallimard.) Divorced from Georgette in July.

1950   Publishes, at Gallimard, *Les Matinaux,* these "poems from my temperate slope," written at Le Rebanqué chez Madame Mathieu. Char helps edit Margerite Caetani's *Botteghe Oscure.*

1951   Meets Nicolas de Staël, about whose work he writes *Bois de Staël; Poèmes,* illustrated with woodcuts by de Staël. In April, *A une Sérénité crispée* (Gallimard), illustrated by Louis Fernandez. Char's mother dies in June.

1952   Éluard dies, and also, Louis Curel (subject of the poem "Louis Curel de la Sorgue").

1953   Publishes *Lettera amorosa,* later illustrated by Braque, and *Le Rempart de brindilles* with engravings by Wifredo Lam.

1955   Publishes *Recherche de la base et du sommet* (Gallimard), first edition of Char's prose texts as a whole, then *Poèmes des deux années* with an etching by Giacometti. Death of de Staël in April. Char meets Heidegger through Jean Beaufret in Paris. The first of three summer visits of the philosopher to the Vaucluse as Char's guest.

In 1956, *La Bibliothèque est en feu,* with an etching by Braque. Boulez' musical setting of *Le Visage nuptial* in Cologne. *Les Compagnons dans le jardin* (Louis Broder), with etchings by Zao Wou-Ki.

1960   Death of Camus; death also of Reverdy, and of Pasternak, with whom Char had been corresponding.

1961   Publishes *L'Inclémence lointaine,* illustrated by Vieira Da Silva (Pierre Bérès). Char buys Les Busclats, a small house on a hill overlooking L'Isle-sur-Sorgue, where he will live for the rest of his life, with frequent stays in Paris.

1962   *La Parole en archipel* (Gallimard) appears, and in 1964, *Commune présence* (Gallimard), poems regrouped by Char according to major themes.

1965   *L'Age cassant* (Corti), appears, and in December, *Retour amont* (G.L.M.) with etchings by Giacometti. Char leads the fight against the implantation of nuclear rockets near the Mont Ventoux (*La Provence point oméga*).

1966   Death of Giacometti in January. Breton dies in the fall.

René Char: Poetry and Passion

The work of René Char . . . is this future word, impersonal and
always yet to come where we hear nevertheless, in the decisiveness of
an originary and intimate language, what is transpiring in the realm
that is the nearest and the most immediate for us.

Maurice Blanchot, "La Bête de Lascaux"

René Char never wanted to separate the terms of poetry and passion. For
him, they were both natural and willed, and their terms were to be expansive
ones. By his writing, his gestures, his mental and emotive choices, and his
continuing impassioned involvement in anything connected with poetry,
René Char never interrupted his lived testimony to the ways in which
reading and writing are deeply moral acts, with consequences. Char's mental
and moral requirements were stringent. A poet radically opposed to limits,
his aim was to enable each reader to walk in the "great spaces of the self," as
he put it to me once. The element of spaciousness was always predominant,
along with that of freedom. That space was to be energized, impassioned by
love and struggle together—thus, his great poems informed equally by both
elements, sometimes even in their titles: "The Nuptial Countenance,"
"Equal Goods," "Mortal Partners," and "Wrestlers." The passion always
implicit in all his poetry passes to the reader as a partner in the creation: to be
disengaged from a text was quite simply not to understand it. Understand-
ing implies the various senses of the poem, some of them developing in this
relation of poem and poet to reader: this is the second sense of the "Nuptial
Countenance," shared also in the reading.

Our first loyalty as readers and translators of Char, in particular, might
well be a faithfulness to his way of seeing. To his speech, so close to our own
poets near at home. William Carlos Williams states his remembrance ("To a
Dog Injured in the Street"):

>   . . . I think
> of the poetry
>   of René Char
>   and all he must have seen

                and suffered
                        that has brought him
                                to speak only of
                sedgy rivers,
                        of daffodils and tulips
                                whose roots they water.

We too must mix strength of statement and of reaction with truth to the text. Our responding commentary and renderings, even under the pressure of emotion—whether that of self or the other—should remain true insofar as possible, in particular to what the poet saw, adding, transforming perhaps, but not deforming to fit any preestablished mode of our own. René Char himself, for example, found a way to "Celebrate Giacometti," specifically through the creative passion of the artist whom he called this "old despotic eagle, the blacksmith kneeling, under the fiery cloud of his own invectives (his work, that is to say, himself, he never ceased to wreak offenses upon it. . . .)" (*Oeuvres Complètes*, 431). *His work, that is to say, himself* . . . It is these words I shall retain, with their basic identification of those two terms signaling some essential violence to which fidelity is no less required. From this violence done to himself comes the primary impulse for Giacometti's work, as it does for Char's own. At the same time, both knew how to remain true to their relations. The title of the collection *Les Voisinages de Van Gogh* speaks of Char's loyalty to these actually or imaginatively close painters and poets, this presence of the other so strongly sensed in his writing, as a countering force to his own violence against himself. That double sense impassions doubly.

   Such moral energy is acquired little by little, still demanding of us that we be ourselves, even as we follow these traces of the poet so closely allied with Provence, its mountains, its rivers, and its ancient *bories* or stone houses.* Built without mortar between their stones, these houses become the allegorical touchstone for poetry. Before Rimbaud, Char maintained, Heraclitus and Georges de La Tour "had built and shown what sort of House

---

   * They had to be followed closely: "See," he used to say to me, "you must keep each word with its face to the wave . . ." In keeping with my belief in the singularity of each struggle, I give an example: the awkward word *bivouaquer*. In English, it seemed to me, the poem would fall flat with such a word, would be a battle-text, unpoetic. But in the world of René Char, such ideas as poetic are not to be given an aura, or to be privileged over others. I finally used the word, with only passing regret. The moral lesson was worth the verbal awkwardness.

among all others humans should inhabit: a dwelling both for the breath and meditation." *(Oeuvres Complètes,* 731) There we learn how to live, read, conceive, and breathe generously, but also, how to leave that dwelling once again, as eventually we must, to set off into this "immensity, this density really made for us." *(Oeuvres Complètes,* 759)

From the early *Le Marteau sans maître,* odd, gleaming, and in the surrealist temper, through the strong and moving poems of the resistance period, that of *Fureur et mystère*—including the war journal *Feuillets d'Hypnos* with its aphoristic wisdom—to the high poetic grace of *Les Matinaux,* the poems of dawning, Char's texts develop a world of their own, yet connected with what is beyond them. By the time of *Le Nu perdu, La Nuit talismanique,* and *Aromates chasseurs,* the mountainous country of the Vaucluse, its luminous wakeful nights and its pungent herbs and legends, is joining its own physical intensity to the metaphysical depths his poetry calls upon and leaves behind. The later *Chants de la Balandrane, Fenêtres dormantes et porte sur le toit, Voisinages de Van Gogh,* and finally *Éloge d'une Soupçonnée* are set at an angle, local and cosmic as always, but with their ellipses and their particularities ringing differently. To read René Char is always, as we readers joined in this volume have learned over the years, to read several aspects of the same unique presence. In each volume, his tone shifts between the oracular and the simple, between sorrowing and rejoicing, between the philosophical and the light. The sense of the profoundly personal mingles with that of the resolutely cosmic, in the voice and being of this poet who knew he spoke for poetry itself, both for its lack and its excess. "The person who comes into the world to disturb nothing," he would say, "is worth neither consideration or patience." And indeed, this could never be said of him. Char's "multiple being" was disturbing, troubling in the highest degree—and the reader is troubled, as Char urgently wished, into poetry. We are summoned immediately to the spontaneous: "Being/at the first leap" and required to accede with our whole being to the possibilities of rethinking both our access routes and our will to arrival. Ease is not predominant here on the heights of the Mont Ventoux, the mountain so close to Char, in so many senses—nothing is settled or easy.

Char is a poet of extremes. It is the essence of his poetry to retain them as well as bridge them, summit and depth. But the bridging itself must retain its own difficulty, psychological and moral: the celebrated text "The Shark and the Seagull" rejects any golden central mean of undetermined character. A unique character is what cannot be compromised:

Yesterday, nobility was a desert, the branch was remote from its buds. The shark and the gull could not communicate.

O rainbow of this gem-cutting shore, bring the ship nearer to its longing. Let every supposed end be a new innocence, a feverish forward march to those stumbling in morning torpor.

We might read this hope for hopefulness, this implicit desire for encounter as allied in essence with the surrealist "state of expectation." Yet the essential fierceness of this poet's Provençal nature must never be overlooked in his work: "Bee-swarm, lightning flash, and absolute condemnation: three oblique angles of one summit." In the moral and psychological universe of Char, as in his poetry, each element must retain its unique and radical difference. Things do not merge into a blurred likeness; they do not compromise each other, or themselves by so doing. Each extreme keeps its extreme nature.

And so it is with translations of René Char, as they meet here, side by side with his words. They do not aspire to identity, rather to a continuity created by and through the things and notions and feelings experienced in some implicit meeting of minds and souls, guaranteeing a ceaselessly acknowledged difference that will keep the sharp profile of each singular entity.

Translation requires, at its origin, a reading as full as possible, with multiplicities inherent in sense and sound often impossible in transcription and yet nourishing the final expression. The special stress of translating this mountainous and splendidly various poet will be clear in the distinct differences among the translators' multiform ways of rendering his diverse tones and his steady intensity, the latter also the source for such continuities and convergences as are found here. Value is matched with value, summits and depths with each other.

"Children and geniuses know that there is no bridge, only the water that lets itself be crossed. So, in Braque, the fountain is inseparable from the rock, the fruit from the ground, the cloud from its fate, invisibly and overwhelmingly . . ." What Char perceived about Braque's work we might perceive in his own, and in our encounter with him. For many of us speaking here in response, that encounter felt fateful. This collective volume intends to bear witness to that experience.

Mary Ann Caws
New York, September 1991

Selected Poems of René Char

Le Marteau sans maître

LA ROSE VIOLENTE

Œil en transe miroir muet
Comme je m'approche je m'éloigne
Bouée au créneau

Tête contre tête tout oublier
Jusqu'au coup d'épaule en plein cœur
La rose violente
Des amants nuls et transcendants.

ARTINE

Au silence de celle qui laisse rêveur.

Dans le lit qu'on m'avait préparé il y avait : un animal sanguinolent et meurtri, de la taille d'une brioche, un tuyau de plomb, une rafale de vent, un coquillage glacé, une cartouche tirée, deux doigts d'un gant, une tache d'huile ; il n'y avait pas de porte de prison, il y avait le goût de l'amertume, un diamant de vitrier, un cheveu, un jour, une chaise cassée, un ver à soie, l'objet volé, une chaîne de pardessus, une mouche verte apprivoisée, une branche de corail, un clou de cordonnier, une roue d'omnibus.

Offrir au passage un verre d'eau à un cavalier lancé à bride abattue sur un hippodrome envahi par la foule suppose, de part et d'autre, un manque absolu d'adresse ; Artine apportait aux esprits qu'elle visitait cette sécheresse monumentale.

L'impatient se rendait parfaitement compte de l'ordre des rêves qui hanteraient dorénavant son cerveau, surtout dans le domaine de l'amour où l'activité dévorante se manifestait couramment en dehors du temps sexuel ; l'assimilation se développant, la nuit noire, dans les serres bien closes.

Artine traverse sans difficulté le nom d'une ville. C'est le silence qui détache le sommeil.

The Hammer with No Master

THE VIOLENT ROSE

Eye in a trance silent mirror
As I approach I depart
Buoy in the battlements

Head against head to forget all
Until the shoulder butts the heart
The violent rose
Of ruined and transcendent lovers.   [PA]

ARTINE

To the silence of one who sets us dreaming.

In the bed prepared for me there were: an animal bruised and slightly bleeding, no larger than a bun, a lead pipe, a gust of wind, an icy seashell, a spent cartridge, two fingers of a glove, a spot of oil; there was no prison gate, rather the taste of bitterness, a glazier's diamond, one hair, one day, a broken chair, a silkworm, the stolen object, an overcoat chain, a tame green fly, a branch of coral, a cobbler's nail, a bus wheel.

To offer a glass of water to a horseman as he passes hurtling headlong on a racetrack invaded by the crowd takes an absolute awkwardness on both sides; Artine brought to the minds she visited this monumental drought.

Impatient, he was perfectly aware of the order of dreams which would henceforth haunt his brain, especially in the realm of love whose devouring activities usually appeared in other than sexual moments: assimilation developing, through the dead of darkness, in greenhouses closed tight.

Artine traverses effortlessly the name of a town. Silence unleashes sleep.

3

Les objets désignés et rassemblés sous le nom de *nature-précise* font partie du décor dans lequel se déroulent les actes d'érotisme des *suites fatales*, épopée quotidienne et nocturne. Les mondes imaginaires chauds qui circulent sans arrêt dans la campagne à l'époque des moissons rendent l'œil agressif et la solitude intolérable à celui qui dispose du pouvoir de destruction. Pour les extraordinaires bouleversements il est tout de même préférable de s'en remettre entièrement à eux.

L'état de léthargie qui précédait Artine apportait les éléments indispensables à la projection d'impressions saisissantes sur l'écran de ruines flottantes: édredon en flammes précipité dans l'insondable gouffre de ténèbres en perpétuel mouvement.

Artine gardait en dépit des animaux et des cyclones une intarissable fraîcheur. À la promenade, c'était la transparence absolue.

A beau surgir au milieu de la plus active dépression l'appareil de la beauté d'Artine, les esprits curieux demeurent des esprits furieux, les esprits indifférents des esprits extrêmement curieux.

Les apparitions d'Artine dépassaient le cadre de ces contrées du sommeil, où le *pour* et le *pour* sont animés d'une égale et meurtrière violence. Elles évoluaient dans les plis d'une soie brûlante peuplée d'arbres aux feuilles de cendre.

La voiture à chevaux lavée et remise à neuf l'emportait presque toujours sur l'appartement tapissé de salpêtre lorsqu'il s'agissait d'accueillir durant une soirée interminable la multitude des ennemis mortels d'Artine. Le visage de bois mort était particulièrement odieux. La course haletante de deux amants au hasard des grands chemins devenait tout à coup une distraction suffisante pour permettre au drame de se dérouler, derechef, à ciel ouvert.

Quelquefois une manœuvre maladroite faisait tomber sur la gorge d'Artine une tête qui n'était pas la mienne. L'énorme bloc de soufre se consumait alors lentement, sans fumée, présence en soi et immobilité vibrante.

Le livre ouvert sur les genoux d'Artine était seulement lisible les jours sombres. À intervalles irréguliers les héros venaient apprendre les malheurs qui allaient à nouveau fondre sur eux, les voies multiples et terrifiantes dans lesquelles leur irréprochable destinée allait à nouveau s'engager. Uniquement soucieux de la Fatalité, ils étaient pour la plupart d'un physique agréable. Ils se déplaçaient avec lenteur, se montraient peu loquaces. Ils exprimaient leurs désirs à l'aide de larges mouvements de tête imprévisibles. Ils paraissaient en outre s'ignorer totalement entre eux.

Le poète a tué son modèle.

The objects described by and gathered under the name of *nature-précise** form part of the setting for erotic acts bound to *fatal consequences,* an epic daily and nocturnal. Hot imaginary worlds circulating ceaselessly in the countryside at harvest-time render the eye aggressive and solitude intolerable to the wielder of destructive power. For extraordinary upheavals, however, it is preferable to rely altogether upon them.

The lethargic state preceding Artine added things indispensable to the projection of striking impressions on the screen of floating ruins: eiderdown in flames cast into the unfathomable abyss of perpetually moving shadows.

In spite of animals and cyclones, Artine retained an inexhaustible freshness. On outings, this was the most absolute transparency.

From the most active depression, the array of Artine's beauty may arise, but the curious minds remain nevertheless furious, the indifferent minds extremely curious.

Artine's appearances went past the border of those countries of sleep where the *for* and the *for* are endowed with an equal and murderous violence. They occurred in the folds of a burning silk peopled with ashen-leaved trees.

Washed and renovated, the horse-drawn chariot nearly always won out over the saltpeter-papered apartment playing host for an interminable evening to the multitude of Artine's mortal enemies. The dead-wood face was particularly odious. The breathless race of two lovers at random along the highways suddenly became diversion sufficient for a dramatic unfolding, then and there, out in the open.

Sometimes, a careless movement caused a head other than mine to sink on Artine's breast. The enormous sulfur block consumed its substance slowly and smokelessly, presence in itself vibrating motionless.

The book open on Artine's knees could be read only on somber days. At irregular intervals heroes would come to learn the calamities once more to befall them, and in what numerous and fearful directions their irreproachable fate would start out afresh. Concerned only with Fatality, they presented for the most part an agreeable appearance. They moved about slowly and were not loquacious. They expressed their desires in broad unforeseable motions of their heads. Moreover, they seemed to be utterly unconscious of each other.

The poet has slain his model.   [MAC]

* Here the term plays on "nature-morte" or still-life.(Tr. note)

LA MAIN DE LACENAIRE

Les mondes éloquents ont été perdus.

L'INSTITUTEUR RÉVOQUÉ

Trois personnages d'une banalité éprouvée s'abordent à des titres poétiques divers (du feu, je vous prie, quelle heure avez-vous, à combien de lieues la prochaine ville?), dans un paysage indifférent et engagent une conversation dont les échos ne nous parviendront jamais. Devant vous, le champ de dix hectares dont je suis le laboureur, le sang secret et la pierre catastrophique. Je ne vous laisse rien à penser.

CHAÎNE

Le grand bûcher des alliances
Sous le spiral ciel d'échec
C'est l'hiver en barque pourrie
Des compagnons solides aux compagnes liquides
Des lits de mort sous les écorces
Dans les profondeurs vacantes de la terre
Les arcs forgent un nouveau nombre d'ailes
Les labours rayonnants adorent les guérisseurs détrempés
Sur la paille des fatalistes
L'écume d'astre coule tout allumée
Il n'y a pas d'absence irremplaçable.

LACENAIRE'S HAND

Worlds of eloquence have been lost.   [PA]

THE FIRED SCHOOLTEACHER

Three characters of proven banality accost each other with diverse poetical phrases (got a match, I beg of you, what time is it, how many leagues to the next town?), in an indifferent countryside and engage in a conversation whose echoes will never reach us. Before you is the twenty-acre field: I am its worker, its secret blood, its catastrophic stone. I leave you nothing to think.

[PA]

CHAIN

The great pyre of alliances
Beneath the spiral sky of failure
In the rotted boat it is winter
From solid companions to liquid partners
Deathbeds below the crust
In the earth's vacant depths
The arcs forge a new number of wings
The bright tillage worships the sodden healers
On the straw of fatalists
The lighted star-foam flows
There is no absence that cannot be replaced.   [PA]

LES OBSERVATEURS ET LES RÊVEURS

à Maurice Blanchard

Avant de rejoindre les nomades
Les séducteurs allument les colonnes de pétrole
Pour dramatiser les récoltes

Demain commenceront les travaux poétiques
Précédés du cycle de la mort volontaire
Le règne de l'obscurité a coulé la raison le diamant dans la mine

Mères éprises des mécènes du dernier soupir
Mères excessives
Toujours à creuser le cœur massif
Sur vous passera indéfiniment le frisson des fougères des cuisses
    embaumées
On vous gagnera
Vous vous coucherez

Seuls aux fenêtres des fleuves
Les grands visages éclairés
Rêvent qu'il n'y a rien de périssable
Dans leur paysage carnassier.

OBSERVERS AND DREAMERS

to Maurice Blanchard

Before rejoining the nomads
The seducers ignite columns of gas
To dramatize the harvest

Poetic toil will begin tomorrow
Preceded by the cycle of voluntary death
The reign of darkness scuttling reason the diamond in the mine

Mothers smitten with patrons of the last sigh
Excessive mothers
Endlessly furrowing the massive heart
Endless prey to the shuddering ferns of embalmed thighs
You will be won
You will go to bed

Alone at river-windows
Great lighted faces
Dream there is nothing that dies
In their carnivorous landscape.   [PA]

Placard pour un chemin des écoliers

COMPAGNIE DE L'ÉCOLIÈRE

Je sais bien que les chemins marchent
Plus vite que les écoliers
Attelés à leur cartable
Roulant dans la glu des fumées
Où l'automne perd le souffle
Jamais douce à vos sujets
Est-ce vous que j'ai vu sourire
Ma fille ma fille je tremble

N'aviez-vous donc pas méfiance
De ce vagabond étranger
Quand il enleva sa casquette
Pour vous demander son chemin
Vous n'avez pas paru surprise
Vous vous êtes abordés
Comme coquelicot et blé
Ma fille ma fille je tremble

La fleur qu'il tient entre les dents
Il pourrait la laisser tomber
S'il consent à donner son nom
À rendre l'épave à ses vagues
Ensuite quelque aveu maudit
Qui hanterait votre sommeil
Parmi les ajoncs de son sang
Ma fille ma fille je tremble

Quand ce jeune homme s'éloigna
Le soir mura votre visage
Quand ce jeune homme s'éloigna
Dos voûté front bas et mains vides

Notice for a Schoolchild's Path

THE SCHOOLGIRL'S COMPANION

I realize that the roads are swift
Unlike the schoolboy traipsing home
With a satchel harnessed to his back
As he wanders through the cloying fumes
Of Autumn in its breathless fall
Though never one for lenience
Was it you I now saw smiling
I tremble for you little daughter

Were you not wary after all
Of this wandering stranger
When raising his cap to you
He asked you the way
You hardly seemed surprised at all
You were drawn to one another like
A poppy to a stalk of corn
I tremble for you little daughter

He holds a flower between his teeth
Yet may well just dispense with it
If willing to reveal his name
Returning the drowned man to the sea
Thereafter some dark constatation
That would haunt you in your sleep
Amid his bloodstream's briar-brake
I tremble for you little daughter

When the young man went on his way
Dusk lay on your face like stone
When the young man went on his way
Back hunched head down hands empty

Sous les osiers vous étiez grave
Vous ne l'aviez jamais été
Vous rendra-t-il votre beauté
Ma fille ma fille je tremble

La fleur qu'il gardait à la bouche
Savez-vous ce qu'elle cachait
Père un mal pur bordé de mouches
Je l'ai voilé de ma pitié
Mais ses yeux tenaient la promesse
Que je me suis faite à moi-même
Je suis folle je suis nouvelle
C'est vous mon père qui changez.

QUATRE ÂGES

II

J'ai étranglé
Mon frère
Parce qu'il n'aimait pas dormir
La fenêtre ouverte

Ma sœur
A-t-il dit avant de mourir
J'ai passé des nuits pleines
À te regarder dormir
Penché sur ton éclat dans la vitre.

Under the willows your face was grave
You had never been that way before
Will he give you back your beauty
I tremble for you little daughter

That flower hanging from his mouth
Do you know what it was hiding
Father a pure evil bordered with flies
I laid my pity on him like a veil
And yet his eyes were equal to
The promise I had made myself
I'm foolish yes I'm newly fledged
It's you my father who are changing.   [MH]

FOUR AGES

II

I strangled
My brother
Because he hated sleeping
With the window open

My sister,
He said, before he died,
I've spent entire nights
Watching you sleeping,
Leaning on your reflection in the window.   [MH]

Dehors la nuit est gouvernée

COURBET: LES CASSEURS DE CAILLOUX

Sable paille ont la vie douce le vin ne s'y brise pas
Du colombier ils récoltent les plumes
De la goulotte ils ont la langue avide
Ils retardent l'orteil des filles
Dont ils percent les chrysalides
Le sang bien souffert tombe dans l'anecdote de leur légèreté

Nous dévorons la peste du feu gris dans la rocaille
Quand on intrigue à la commune
C'est encore sur les chemins ruinés qu'on est le mieux
Là les tomates des vergers l'air nous les porte au crépuscule
Avec l'oubli de la méchanceté prochaine de nos femmes
Et l'aigreur de la soif tassée aux genoux

Fils cette nuit nos travaux de poussière
Seront visibles dans le ciel
Déjà l'huile du plomb ressuscite.

Outside the Night Is Ruled

COURBET: THE STONE BREAKERS

Sand straw live softly softly take the wine
Gather the down-drifting dovecot feathers
Parch with the avid water-channel
Stay girls barefoot going
Pierce their chrysalids
Drink lightly carelessly the well suffered blood

We devour the grey fire's pest among the stones
While in the village they plot and plan
The best place still for men is the ruined roads
The tomatoes in the garden are borne to us on the twilight air
And of our women's next spite forgetfulness
And the smart of thirst aching in our knees

Sons this night our labor of dust
Will be visible in the sky
Already the oil rises from the lead again.*

---

* According to André du Bouchet this translation, first published in *Transition Forty-nine,* is to be attributed to Samuel Beckett. (Ed. note)

Fureur et mystère

"L'HOMME FUIT L'ASPHYXIE."

1938

L'homme fuit l'asphyxie.

L'homme dont l'appétit hors de l'imagination se calfeutre sans finir de s'approvisionner, se délivrera par les mains, rivières soudainement grossies.

L'homme qui s'épointe dans la prémonition, qui déboise son silence intérieur et le répartit en théâtres, ce second c'est le faiseur de pain.

Aux uns la prison et la mort. Aux autres la transhumance du Verbe.

Déborder l'économie de la création, agrandir le sang des gestes, devoir de toute lumière.

Nous tenons l'anneau où sont enchaînés côte à côte, d'une part le rossignol diabolique, d'autre part la clé angélique.

Sur les arêtes de notre amertume, l'aurore de la conscience s'avance et dépose son limon.

Aoûtement. Une dimension franchit le fruit de l'autre. Dimensions adversaires. Déporté de l'attelage et des noces, je bats le fer des fermoirs invisibles.

CONGÉ AU VENT

À flancs de coteau du village bivouaquent des champs fournis de mimosas. À l'époque de la cueillette, il arrive que, loin de leur endroit, on fasse la rencontre extrêmement odorante d'une fille dont les bras se sont occupés durant la journée aux fragiles branches. Pareille à une lampe dont l'auréole de clarté serait de parfum, elle s'en va, le dos tourné au soleil couchant.

Il serait sacrilège de lui adresser la parole.

L'espadrille foulant l'herbe, cédez-lui le pas du chemin. Peut-être aurez-vous la chance de distinguer sur ses lèvres la chimère de l'humidité de la Nuit?

Furor and Mystery

"MAN FLEES SUFFOCATION."

1938

Man flees suffocation.

Man, whose appetite beyond imagination shuts himself up in laying supplies, will find freedom by his hands, rivers suddenly swollen.

Man who grows blunt through premonitions, who deforests his inner silence and divides it into stages, the latter one is the maker of bread.

To the former, prison and death. To the latter, the repasturing of the Word.

To exceed the economy of creation, to increase the blood of gestures, task of all light.

We hold the ring where the devilish nightingale and the angelic key are chained together, side by side.

Over the ridge of our bitterness, the dawn of conscience comes forth to deposit its loam.

August ripening. One dimension traverses the fruit of the other. Warring dimensions. Deported from the yoke and from the nuptials, I strike the iron of invisible hinges.   [MAC]

WIND AWAY

Camped on the hillsides near the village are fields of mimosa. During the gathering season, it may happen that, some distance away, you meet an extremely sweet smelling girl whose arms have been busy during the day among the fragile branches. Like a lamp with a bright nimbus of perfume, she goes her way, her back to the setting sun.

To speak to her would be sacrilege.

The grass crushed beneath her slippers. Give her right of way. You may be lucky enough to make out on her lips the chimaera of the damp of Night.

[DD & JM]

LA COMPAGNE DU VANNIER

Je t'aimais. J'aimais ton visage de source raviné par l'orage et le chiffre de ton domaine enserrant mon baiser. Certains se confient à une imagination toute ronde. Aller me suffit. J'ai rapporté du désespoir un panier si petit, mon amour, qu'on a pu le tresser en osier.

FRÉQUENCE

Tout le jour, assistant l'homme, le fer a appliqué son torse sur la boue enflammée de la forge. À la longue, leurs jarrets jumeaux ont fait éclater la mince nuit du métal à l'étroit sous la terre.

L'homme sans se hâter quitte le travail. Il plonge une dernière fois ses bras dans le flanc assombri de la rivière. Saura-t-il enfin saisir le bourdon glacé des algues?

JEUNESSE

Loin de l'embuscade des tuiles et de l'aumône des calvaires, vous vous donnez naissance, otages des oiseaux, fontaines. La pente de l'homme faite de la nausée de ses cendres, de l'homme en lutte avec sa providence vindicative, ne suffit pas à vous désenchanter.

Éloge, nous nous sommes acceptés.

"Si j'avais été muette comme la marche de pierre fidèle au soleil et qui ignore sa blessure cousue de lierre, si j'avais été enfant comme l'arbre blanc qui accueille les frayeurs des abeilles, si les collines avaient vécu jusqu'à l'été, si l'éclair m'avait ouvert sa grille, si tes nuits m'avaient pardonné . . ."

Regard, verger d'étoiles, les genêts, la solitude sont distincts de vous! Le chant finit l'exil. La brise des agneaux ramène la vie neuve.

THE BASKET-WEAVER'S LOVE

I loved you. I loved your face, a spring furrowed by storm, and the emblem of your domain enclosing my kiss. Some put their trust in a round imagination. Just going is enough for me. I brought back from despair so small a basket, my love, they wove it of willow.   [MAC & PT]

FREQUENCY

All day long, helping out, the iron leaned its torso against the flaming mire of the forge. Finally, their twin hocks shattered the thin night of the metal so tightly confined in the earth.

The man without haste leaves his work. One last time his arms plunge into the darkened flank of the river. Will he finally grasp the icy bell-shaped algae?   [MAC & PT]

YOUTH

Far from the ambush of roofs and the alms of country shrines you take your birth, hostages of the birds, O fountains. Man's decline in the nausea of his ashes, man's struggle with his vindictive providence, not even these can disillusion you.

Praise, praise, we have come to terms with ourselves.

"If I had been mute as the trusty stone step beneath the sun heedless of its wound sewn with ivy," she said, "if I had been childlike as the white tree receiving the fright of bees, if the hills had lived on into summer, if the lightning had opened its gates to me, if your night had forgiven me . . ."

Eyes, the orchard of stars, the gorse, the solitude are not part of you. A song finishes exile. The lamb-wind brings back new life.   [DD & JM]

LE LORIOT

3 septembre 1939

Le loriot entra dans la capitale de l'aube.
L'épée de son chant ferma le lit triste.
Tout à jamais prit fin.

L'ABSENT

Ce frère brutal mais dont la parole était sûre, patient au sacrifice, diamant et sanglier, ingénieux et secourable, se tenait au centre de tous les malentendus tel un arbre de résine dans le froid inalliable. Au bestiaire de mensonges qui le tourmentait de ses gobelins et de ses trombes il opposait son dos perdu dans le temps. Il venait à vous par des sentiers invisibles, favorisait l'audace écarlate, ne vous contrariait pas, savait sourire. Comme l'abeille quitte le verger pour le fruit déjà noir, les femmes soutenaient sans le trahir le paradoxe de ce visage qui n'avait pas des traits d'otage.

J'ai essayé de vous décrire ce compère indélébile que nous sommes quelques-uns à avoir fréquenté. Nous dormirons dans l'espérance, nous dormirons en son absence, puisque la raison ne soupçonne pas que ce qu'elle nomme, à la légère, absence, occupe le fourneau dans l'unité.

THE ORIOLE

3 September 1939

The oriole entered the capital of dawn.
The blade of his song closed the bed of sorrow.
All ended forever. [JM]

THE ABSENT ONE

This brutal brother but whose word was true, steadfast in the face of sacrifice, diamond and wild boar, ingenious and helpful, held himself in the center of all misunderstandings like a resinous tree in the cold admitting of no alloy. Against the bestiary of lies tormenting him with its goblins and its whirlwinds, he set his back, lost in time. He came to you by invisible paths, preferred a scarlet forwardness, did not thwart you, knew how to smile. As the bee leaves the orchard for the fruit already black, women withstood without betraying it the paradox of this face which had none of the lineaments of a hostage.

I have tried to describe for you this indelible companion whose friendship some of us have kept. We shall sleep in hope, we shall sleep in his absence, reason not suspecting that what it names, thoughtlessly, absence, dwells within the crucible of unity. [MAC]

21

L'ÉPI DE CRISTAL ÉGRÈNE DANS LES HERBES
SA MOISSON TRANSPARENTE

La ville n'était pas défaite. Dans la chambre devenue légère le donneur de liberté couvrait son amour de cet immense effort du corps, semblable à celui de la création d'un fluide par le jour. L'alchimie du désir rendait essentiel leur génie récent à l'univers de ce matin. Loin derrière eux leur mère ne les trahirait plus, leur mère si immobile. Maintenant ils précédaient le pays de leur avenir qui ne contenait encore que la flèche de leur bouche dont le chant venait de naître. Leur avidité rencontrait immédiatement son objet. Ils douaient d'omniprésence un temps qu'on n'interrogeait pas.

Il lui disait comment jadis dans des forêts persécutées il interpellait les animaux auxquels il apportait leur chance, son serment aux monts internés qui l'avait conduit à la reconnaissance de son exemplaire destin et quel boucher secret il avait dû vaincre pour acquérir à ses yeux la tolérance de son semblable.

Dans la chambre devenue légère et qui peu à peu développait les grands espaces du voyage, le donneur de liberté s'apprêtait à disparaître, à se confondre avec d'autres naissances, une nouvelle fois.

CHANT DU REFUS

Début du partisan

Le poète est retourné pour de longues années dans le néant du père. Ne l'appelez pas, vous tous qui l'aimez. S'il vous semble que l'aile de l'hirondelle n'a plus de miroir sur terre, oubliez ce bonheur. Celui qui panifiait la souffrance n'est pas visible dans sa léthargie rougeoyante.

Ah! beauté et vérité fassent que vous soyez *présents* nombreux aux salves de la délivrance!

THE CRYSTAL WHEAT-EAR SHEDS IN THE GRASSES
ITS TRANSPARENT HARVEST

The town was not undone. In the room become weightless, the bestower of freedom covered his beloved with this immense effort of the body, akin to a fluid's creation by the day. Desire in its alchemy rendered their recent genius essential to that morning's universe. Far behind them, their mother would betray them no more, their mother so unmoving. Now they preceded the country of their future which contained as yet only the arrow of their mouth whose song had just been born. Their avidity met its object straightaway. They endowed with omnipresence a time free of questioning.

He told her how in days gone by, in the persecuted forests, he would summon animals to whom he brought their chance, how his oath to the imprisoned mountains had made him recognize his exemplary fate and what secret butcher he'd had to conquer before winning in his own eyes his fellow-man's tolerance.

In the room become weightless and gradually unfurling vast expanses of voyage, the bestower of freedom readied himself to disappear, to mingle with other births, once again.   [MAC]

REFUSAL SONG

Beginning of the Partisan

The poet has returned for a long span of years into the naught of the father. Do not call him, all you who love him. If it seems to you that the swallow's wing has no longer a mirror on earth, forget that happiness. He who worked suffering into bread is not visible in his glowing lethargy.

Ah! may beauty and truth ensure your numerous *presence* at the salvos of liberation!   [MAC]

HOMMAGE ET FAMINE

Femme qui vous accordez avec la bouche du poète, ce torrent au limon serein, qui lui avez appris, alors qu'il n'était encore qu'une graine captive de loup anxieux, la tendresse des hauts murs polis par votre nom (hectares de Paris, entrailles de beauté, mon feu monte sous vos robes de fugue), Femme qui dormez dans le pollen des fleurs, déposez sur son orgueil votre givre de médium illimité, afin qu'il demeure jusqu'à l'heure de la bruyère d'ossements l'homme qui pour mieux vous adorer reculait indéfiniment en vous la diane de sa naissance, le poing de sa douleur, l'horizon de sa victoire.

(Il faisait nuit. Nous nous étions serrés sous le grand chêne de larmes. Le grillon chanta. Comment savait-il, solitaire, que la terre n'allait pas mourir, que nous, les enfants sans clarté, allions bientôt parler?)

LA LIBERTÉ

Elle est venue par cette ligne blanche pouvant tout aussi bien signifier l'issue de l'aube que le bougeoir du crépuscule.

Elle passa les grèves machinales; elle passa les cimes éventrées.

Prenaient fin la renonciation à visage de lâche, la sainteté du mensonge, l'alcool du bourreau.

Son verbe ne fut pas un aveugle bélier mais la toile où s'inscrivit mon souffle.

D'un pas à ne se mal guider que derrière l'absence, elle est venue, cygne sur la blessure, par cette ligne blanche.

HOMAGE AND FAMINE

Woman atune to the mouth of the poet, this torrent with serene alluvium, who taught him, when he was only a captive seed of anxious wolf, the tenderness of high walls burnished by your name (acres of Paris, entrails of beauty, my fire rises under your dresses of fugue), Woman sleeping in flower pollen, lay lightly on his pride your frost of limitless medium, that he remain until the hour of the heather of bones the man who the better to adore you thrust back unendingly in you the clarion of his birth, the fist of his suffering, the horizon of his victory.

(It was night. We were huddled under the great oak of tears. The cricket chirped. How did he know, solitary, that the earth was not to die, that we, children without clarity, were soon to speak?)   [MAC]

FREEDOM

It came along this white line that might signify dawn's emergence as well as dusk's candlestick.

It passed beyond the unconscious strands; it passed beyond the eviscerated summits.

They were ending: the cowardly countenanced renunciation, the holiness of lying, the harsh drink of the executioner.

Its word was not a blind battering-ram but rather the canvas where my breath was inscribed.

With a pace unsure only behind absence, it came, a swan on the wound, along this white line.   [MAC]

CONDUITE

Passe.
La bêche sidérale
autrefois là s'est engouffrée.
Ce soir un village d'oiseaux
très haut exulte et passe.

Écoute aux tempes rocheuses
des présences dispersées
le mot qui fera ton sommeil
chaud comme un arbre de septembre.

Vois bouger l'entrelacement
des certitudes arrivées
près de nous à leur quintessence,
ô ma Fourche, ma Soif anxieuse!

La rigueur de vivre se rode
sans cesse à convoiter l'exil.
Par une fine pluie d'amande,
mêlée de liberté docile,
ta gardienne alchimie s'est produite,
ô Bien-aimée!

CONVEY

Pass.
The sidereal spade
Long ago struck in there.
Tonight a high village of birds
Exults and passes.

Listen at the stony temples
of presences dispersed
to the word making your sleep
warm as a September tree.

Mark the moving of the interwoven certainties
that beside us have attained
their quintessence,
o my Cleaving, my anxious Thirst!

The rigor of living ceaselessly
Wears down, coveting exile.
Through a fine rain of almond,
mingled with gentle liberty,
your guardian alchemy has done its work,
o Beloved!   [MAC]

LE VISAGE NUPTIAL

A présent disparais, mon escorte, debout dans la distance;
La douceur du nombre vient de se détruire.
Congé à vous, mes alliés, mes violents, mes indices.
Tout vous entraîne, tristesse obséquieuse.
J'aime.

L'eau est lourde à un jour de la source.
La parcelle vermeille franchit ses lentes branches à ton front, dimension
rassurée.
Et moi semblable à toi,
Avec la paille en fleur au bord du ciel criant ton nom,
J'abats les vestiges,
Atteint, sain de clarté.

Ceinture de vapeur, multitude assouplie, diviseurs de la crainte, touchez ma
renaissance.
Parois de ma durée, je renonce à l'assistance de ma largeur vénielle;
Je boise l'expédient du gîte, j'entrave la primeur des survies.
Embrasé de solitude foraine,
J'évoque la nage sur l'ombre de sa Présence.

Le corps désert, hostile à son mélange, hier, était revenu parlant noir.
Déclin, ne te ravise pas, tombe ta massue de transes, aigre sommeil.
Le décolleté diminue les ossements de ton exil, de ton escrime;
Tu rends fraîche la servitude qui se dévore le dos;
Risée de la nuit, arrête ce charroi lugubre
De voix vitreuses, de départs lapidés.

Tôt soustrait au flux des lésions inventives
(La pioche de l'aigle lance haut le sang évasé)
Sur un destin présent j'ai mené mes franchises
Vers l'azur multivalve, la granitique dissidence.

THE NUPTIAL COUNTENANCE

Now let my escort disappear, standing in the distance;
numbers have just lost their sweetness.
I give you leave, my allies, my violent ones, my indices.
Everything summons you away, fawning sorrow.
I am in love.

Water is heavy at a day's flow from the spring.
The crimson foliage crosses its slow branches at your forehead, dimension
    reassured.
And I, like you,
with the straw in flower at the edge of the sky crying your name,
I cut down the traces,
stricken, strong in clarity.

Ring of vapor, many made supple, dividers of fear, touch my renewal.
Walls of my enduring, I renounce the succor of my venial breadth;
I timber the device of the dwelling, I thwart the first fruits of survivals.
Afire with itinerant solitude,
I evoke the swimming on the shade of her Presence.

The desert body hostile to an alloyage, had returned yesterday, speaking
    darkly.
Decline, do not halt your movement, drop your bludgeon of seizures, acrid
    sleep.
Indentation diminishes the bones of your exile, of your sparring;
you freshen constraint self-devouring;
gust of the night, halt this grim cartage
of glazed voices, stone-pelted departures.

Soon subtracted from the flux of contriving lesions
(the eagle's pickaxe flings high the flaring blood)
across a present destiny I have led my exemptions
toward an azure multivalved, granite dissidence.

29

Ô voûte d'effusion sur la couronne de son ventre,
Murmure de dot noire!
Ô mouvement tari de sa diction!
Nativité, guidez les insoumis, qu'ils découvrent leur base,
L'amande croyable au lendemain neuf.
Le soir a fermé sa plaie de corsaire où voyageaient les fusées vagues parmi la
    peur soutenue des chiens.
Au passé les micas du deuil sur ton visage.

Vitre inextinguible: mon souffle affleurait déjà l'amitié de ta blessure,
Armait ta royauté inapparente.
Et des lèvres du brouillard descendit notre plaisir au seuil de dune, au toit
    d'acier.
La conscience augmentait l'appareil frémissant de ta permanence;
La simplicité fidèle s'étendit partout.

Timbre de la devise matinale, morte-saison de l'étoile précoce,
Je cours au terme de mon cintre, colisée fossoyé.
Assez baisé le crin nubile des céréales:
La cardeuse, l'opiniâtre, nos confins la soumettent.
Assez maudit le havre des simulacres nuptiaux:
Je touche le fond d'un retour compact.

Ruisseaux, neume des morts anfractueux,
Vous qui suivez le ciel aride,
Mêlez votre acheminement aux orages de qui sut guérir de la désertion,
Donnant contre vos études salubres.
Au sein du toit le pain suffoque à porter coeur et lueur.
Prends, ma Pensée, la fleur de ma main pénétrable,
Sens s'éveiller l'obscure plantation.

O vaulted effusion upon the crown of her belly,
murmurings of dark dowry!
O the exhausted motion of her diction!
Nativity, guide the unyielding, may they find their foundations,
the almond believable in the fresh day to come.
Evening has closed its corsair's gash where the rockets soared aimlessly amid
a dogged fear.
Past now the micas of mourning on your face.

Unquenchable pane: my breath was already grazing the friendship of your
wound,
arming your hidden royalty.
And from the lips of the fog descended our joy with its threshold of dune, its
roof of steel.
Awareness increased the quivering array of your permanence;
faithful simplicity spread everywhere.

Tone of morning's adage, slack season of the early star,
I rush to the term of my arch, interred coliseum.
Long enough embraced the nubile hair of grain:
O stubborn one, carder, our reaches force its submission.
Long enough condemned the haven of nuptial semblances:
I touch the depths of a compact return.

Streams, neuma of the craggy dead,
you who follow the arid sky,
mingle your going with his storms, who could heal desertion,
striking against your saving studies.
At the roof's center bread suffocates carrying heart and light.
Take, oh my Thought, the flower of my penetrable hand,
Feel the dark planting waken.

Je ne verrai pas tes flancs, ces essaims de faim, se dessécher, s'emplir de
   ronces;
Je ne verrai pas l'empuse te succéder dans ta serre;
Je ne verrai pas l'approche des baladins inquiéter le jour renaissant;
Je ne verrai pas la race de notre liberté servilement se suffire.

Chimères, nous sommes montés au plateau.
Le silex frissonnait sous les sarments de l'espace;
La parole, lasse de défoncer, buvait au débarcadère angélique.
Nulle farouche survivance:
L'horizon des routes jusqu'à l'afflux de rosée,
L'intime dénouement de l'irréparable.

Voici le sable mort, voici le corps sauvé:
La Femme respire, l'Homme se tient debout.

I shall not see your sides, those swarms of hunger, dry up, fill with
    brambles;
I shall not see the mantis replace you in your greenhouse;
I shall not see the minstrels approach, disquieting the reborn day;
I shall not see our freedom's lineage servile in self-sufficiency.

Chimeras, we have climbed upland.
Flint quivered beneath vine-shoots of space;
the word, tired of battering, drank at the angelic wharf.
No savage survival:
the horizon of roads to the abounding dew,
intimate unfolding of the irreparable.

This is the sand dead, this the body saved:
Woman breathes, Man stands upright.   [MAC]

ÉVADNÉ

L'été et notre vie étions d'un seul tenant
La campagne mangeait la couleur de ta jupe odorante
Avidité et contrainte s'étaient réconciliées
Le château de Maubec s'enfonçait dans l'argile
Bientôt s'effondrerait le roulis de sa lyre
La violence des plantes nous faisait vaciller
Un corbeau rameur sombre déviant de l'escadre
Sur le muet silex de midi écartelé
Accompagnait notre entente aux mouvements tendres
La faucille partout devait se reposer
Notre rareté commençait un règne
(Le vent insomnieux qui nous ride la paupière
En tournant chaque nuit la page consentie
Veut que chaque part de toi que je retienne
Soit étendue à un pays d'âge affamé et de larmier géant)

C'était au début d'adorables années
La terre nous aimait un peu je me souviens.

EVADNE

Summer and our life, we were continuous
The country devoured the color of your sweet-smelling skirt
Avidity and constraint had been reconciled
Maubec Castle was settling in the clay
Soon the rolling of its lyre would cease
The violence of plants made us reel
A crow somber rower swerving from the fleet
On the mute flint of quartered noon
Accompanied our understanding with tender movements
Everywhere the sickle must have been at rest
Our rarity began a reign
(The sleepless wind rippling our eyelids
Turning each night the page consented
Wishes any part of you I retain
To extend in a land of famished age and high tear-stone)

This was at the outset of adorable years
The earth loved us a little I remember.   [MAC]

POST-SCRIPTUM

Écartez-vous de moi qui patiente sans bouche;
À vos pieds je suis né, mais vous m'avez perdu;
Mes feux ont trop précisé leur royaume;
Mon trésor a coulé contre votre billot.

Le désert comme asile au seul tison suave
Jamais ne m'a nommé, jamais ne m'a rendu.

Écartez-vous de moi qui patiente sans bouche:
Le trèfle de la passion est de fer dans ma main.

Dans la stupeur de l'air où s'ouvrent mes allées,
Le temps émondera peu à peu mon visage,
Comme un cheval sans fin dans un labour aigri.

PÉNOMBRE

J'étais dans une de ces forêts où le soleil n'a pas accès mais où, la nuit, les
étoiles pénètrent. Ce lieu n'avait le permis d'exister, que parce que l'inquisi-
tion des États l'avait négligé. Les servitudes abandonnées me marquaient
leur mépris. La hantise de punir m'était retirée. Par endroit, le souvenir
d'une force caressait la fugue paysanne de l'herbe. Je me gouvernais sans
doctrine, avec une véhémence sereine. J'étais l'égal de choses dont le secret
tenait sous le rayon d'une aile. Pour la plupart, l'essentiel n'est jamais né, et
ceux qui le possèdent ne peuvent l'échanger sans se nuire. Nul ne consent à
perdre ce qu'il a conquis à la pointe de sa peine! Autrement ce serait la
jeunesse et la grâce, source et delta auraient la même pureté.

J'étais dans une de ces forêts où le soleil n'a pas accès mais où, la nuit, les
étoiles pénètrent pour d'implacables hostilités.

POSTSCRIPT

Stand you away from me who wait nor speak;
I was born at your feet but you have lost me;
Too well my flames have marked their kingdom out;
My treasure sank that struck your chopping-block.

The desert where the one firebrand took refuge
Has never called me out, nor given me up.

Stand you away from me who wait nor speak:
The clover of passion is iron in my hand.

In the dazed air through which I go my ways,
Time will clean up my face, little by little,
Like a horse aimless at his bitter plowing.   [DD & JM]

PENUMBRA

I was in one of those forests where the sun has no access, but where stars penetrate by night. This place could exist only because the inquisition of the State had overlooked it. Forsaken easements showed me their scorn. The obsession to chastise was taken from me. Here and there, the memory of a strength caressed the peasant flights of the grass. I ruled myself without doctrine, in serene vehemence. I was the equal of things whose secret fitted under the beam of a wing. For most, the essential is never born, and its possessors cannot exchange it without harm to themselves. None consents to lose what was conquered by dint of pain! Otherwise, it would be youth and grace, spring and delta would be equally pure.

I was in one of those forests where the sun has no access, but where stars penetrate by night for a relentless warring.   [MAC]

"REDONNEZ-LEUR . . ."

Redonnez-leur ce qui n'est plus présent en eux,
Ils reverront le grain de la moisson s'enfermer dans l'épi et s'agiter sur
    l'herbe.
Apprenez-leur, de la chute à l'essor, les douze mois de leur visage,
Ils chériront le vide de leur cœur jusqu'au désir suivant;
Car rien ne fait naufrage ou ne se plaît aux cendres;
Et qui sait voir la terre aboutir à des fruits,
Point ne l'émeut l'échec quoiqu'il ait tout perdu.

ARGUMENT

Comment vivre sans inconnu devant soi?

Les hommes d'aujourd'hui veulent que le poème soit à l'image de leur vie, faite de si peu d'égards, de si peu d'espace et brûlée d'intolérance.

Parce qu'il ne leur est plus loisible d'agir suprêmement, dans cette préoccupation fatale de se détruire par son semblable, parce que leur inerte richesse les freine et les enchaîne, les hommes d'aujourd'hui, l'instinct affaibli, perdent, tout en se gardant vivants, jusqu'à la poussière de leur nom.

Né de l'appel du devenir et de l'angoisse de la rétention, le poème, s'élevant de son puits de boue et d'étoiles, témoignera presque silencieusement, qu'il n'était rien en lui qui n'existât vraiment ailleurs, dans ce rebelle et solitaire monde des contradictions.

"RESTORE TO THEM . . ."

Restore to them what is no more present in them,
They will see again the harvest grain enclosed in the stalk and swaying
    on the grass.
Teach them, from the fall to the soaring, the twelve months of their face,
They will cherish their emptiness until their heart's next desire;
For nothing is shipwrecked or delights in ashes;
And for the one who can see the earth's fruitful end,
Failure is of no moment, even if all is lost.   [MAC]

ARGUMENT

How can we live without the unknown in front of us?

Those of today want the poem to be in the image of their lives, composed of such little consideration, of such little space, and burned with intolerance.

Because it is no longer given to them to act supremely, in this fatal preoccupation with self-destruction by their fellows, because their inert wealth holds them back and enslaves them, those of today, their instinct weakened, lose—still keeping alive—even the dust of their names.

Born from the summons of becoming and from the anguish of retention, the poem rising from its well of mud and of stars, will bear witness, almost silently, that it contained nothing which did not truly exist elsewhere, in this rebellious and solitary world of contradictions.   [MAC]

LES TROIS SŒURS

Mon amour à la robe de phare bleu,
je baise la fièvre de ton visage
où couche la lumière qui jouit en secret.

J'aime et je sanglote. Je suis vivant
et c'est ton cœur cette Etoile du Matin
à la durée victorieuse qui rougit avant
de rompre le combat des Constellations.

Hors de toi, que ma chair devienne la voile
qui répugne au vent.

I

Dans l'urne des temps secondaires
L'enfant à naître était de craie.
La marche fourchue des saisons
Abritait d'herbe l'inconnu.

La connaissance divisible
Pressait d'averses le printemps.
Un aromate de pays
Prolongeait la fleur apparue.

Communication qu'on outrage,
Ecorce ou givre déposés;
L'air investit, le sang attise;
L'œil fait mystère du baiser.

Donnant vie à la route ouverte,
Le tourbillon vint aux genoux;
Et cet élan, le lit des larmes
S'en emplit d'un seul battement.

THE THREE SISTERS

My love with the blue beacon gown,
I kiss the fever of your face
where lies the light that secretly joys.

I love and I sob, I am living
and your heart is this Morning Star
lasting victorious that blushes before
it ends the combat of the Constellations.

Apart from you, may my flesh become the sail
that shrinks from the wind.

I

In the urn of the secondary age
The child to be born was of chalk.
The forked march of the seasons
Sheltered the unknown with grass.

Severable knowledge pressed
The spring with sudden showers.
An aromatic of the countryside
Prolonged the visible flower.

Communication desecrate,
Deposits of bark or frost;
Air beleaguers, blood inflames;
The eye makes a mystery of the kiss.

Giving life to the open road,
The whirlwind reached to the knees;
And with this urge, the bed of tears
Was filled in a single throb.

La seconde crie et s'évade
De l'abeille ambiante et du tilleul vermeil.
Elle est un jour de vent perpétuel,
Le dé bleu du combat, le guetteur qui sourit
Quand sa lyre profère : "Ce que je veux, sera."

C'est l'heure de se taire,
De devenir la tour
Que l'avenir convoite.

Le chasseur de soi fuit sa maison fragile :
Son gibier le suit n'ayant plus peur.

Leur clarté est si haute, leur santé si nouvelle,
Que ces deux qui s'en vont sans rien signifier
Ne sentent pas les sœurs les ramener à elles
D'un long bâillon de cendre aux forêts blanches.

III

Cet enfant sur ton épaule
Est ta chance et ton fardeau.
Terre en quoi l'orchidée brûle,
Ne le fatiguez pas de vous.

Restez fleur et frontière,
Restez manne et serpent;
Ce que la chimère accumule
Bientôt délaisse le refuge.

Meurent les yeux singuliers
Et la parole qui découvre.
La plaie qui rampe au miroir
Est maîtresse des deux bouges.

Violente l'épaule s'entrouve;
Muet apparaît le volcan.
Terre sur quoi l'olivier brille,
Tout s'évanouit en passage.

II

The second cries and flees
The encompassing bee and the red lime-tree.
She is a day of unceasing wind,
The blue die of combat, the watcher who smiles
When his lyre utters: "What I will, shall be."

It is the hour to be silent,
To turn into the tower
That the future covets.

The hunter of self flees his frail house :
No longer fearful, his game follows after.

Their clarity is so high, their health so new,
That these two setting out void of meaning
Do not feel the sisters draw them back
By a long ashen silence to the white forests.

III

This child on your shoulder
Is your fortune and your burden.
Earth in which the orchid burns,
Do not weary him of you.

Remain flower and boundary,
Remain manna and serpent;
What the chimera amasses
Soon forsakes the shelter.

May strange eyes die
And the word that discovers.
The wound that crawls in the mirror
Is mistress of both dens.

Violent the shoulder gapes;
Mute appears the volcano.
Earth on which the olive-tree gleams,
Everything swoons into transiency.   [EJ]

SEUIL

Quand s'ébranla le barrage de l'homme, aspiré par la faille géante de l'abandon du divin, des mots dans le lointain, des mots qui ne voulaient pas se perdre, tentèrent de résister à l'exorbitante poussée. Là se décida la dynastie de leur sens.

J'ai couru jusqu'à l'issue de cette nuit diluvienne. Planté dans le flageolant petit jour, ma ceinture pleine de saisons, je vous attends, ô mes amis qui allez venir. Déjà je vous devine derrière la noirceur de l'horizon. Mon âtre ne tarit pas de vœux pour vos maisons. Et mon bâton de cyprès rit de tout son cœur pour vous.

THRESHOLD

When the barrage of man gave way, caught up in the gigantic rift, the forsaking of the divine, words in the distance, words which were loath to be lost, tried to resist the excessive thrust. It was here the dynasty of their meaning was determined.

I have run to the very end of this diluvian night. Planted in the quaking morn, my belt filled with seasons, I await you, my friends who are coming. Already I sense you behind the blackness of the horizon. My hearthstone never tires of wishing your houses well, and my cypress stick laughs gladly for you.   [EJ]

L'EXTRAVAGANT

Il ne déplaçait pas d'ombre en avançant, traduisant une audace tôt consumée, bien que son pas fût assez vulgaire. Ceux qui, aux premières heures de la nuit, ratent leur lit et le perdent ensuite de vue jusqu'au lendemain, peuvent être tentés par les similitudes. Ils cherchent à s'extraire de quelques pierres trop sages, trop chaudes, veulent se délivrer de l'emprise des cristaux à prétention fabuleuse, que la morne démarche du quotidien sécrète, aux lieux de son choix, avec des attouchements de suaire. Tel n'était pas ce marcheur que le voile du paysage lunaire, très bas, semblait ne pas gêner dans son mouvement. Le gel furieux effleurait la surface de son front sans paraître *personnel*. Une route qui s'allonge, un sentier qui dévie sont conformes à l'élan de la pensée qui fredonne. Par la nuit d'hiver fantastiquement propre parce qu'elle était commune à la généralité des habitants de l'univers qui ne la pénétraient pas, le dernier comédien n'allait plus exister. Il avait perdu tout lien avec le volume ancien des sources propices aux interrogations, avec les corps heureux qu'il s'était plu à animer auprès du sien lorsqu'il pouvait encore assigner une cime à son plaisir, une neige à son talent. Aujourd'hui il rompait avec la tristesse devenue un objet aguerri, avec la frayeur du convenu. La terre avait faussé sa persuasion, la terre, de sa vitesse un peu courte, avec son imagination safranée, son usure crevassée par les actes des monstres. Personne n'aurait à l'oublier car l'utile ne l'avait pas assisté, ne l'avait pas dessiné en entier au regard des autres. Sur le plafond de chaux blanche de sa chambre, quelques oiseaux étaient passés mais leur éclair avait fondu dans son sommeil.

Le voile du paysage lunaire maintenant très haut déploie ses couleurs aromatiques au-dessus du personnage que je dis. Il sort éclairé du froid et tourne à jamais le dos au printemps qui n'existe pas.

THE EXTRAVAGANT ONE

He displaced no shadow in his advance, betraying an audacity soon burned out, although his step was rather commonplace. Those who miss their beds in the night's early hours and then lose sight of them until the morrow may be tempted by resemblances. They try to break away from stones too wise, too warm, wishing to escape from the hold of crystals of fabulous claim which daily usage secretes, in places of its choosing, with a shroud's light touch. Such was not this man who appeared to be unhindered by the low-hanging veil of the lunar landscape. The raging frost brushed his forehead lightly without seeming *personal*. A road extending, a path diverging are consistent with the forward thrust of thought humming. In the winter night miraculously clean, because it was common to those dwelling in the universe who did not penetrate into it, the last player would no longer exist. He had lost every tie with the ancient swell of springs favorable to questioning, with the joyous bodies he had pleased to quicken near his own when he could still assign a summit to his pleasure, a snowfall to his talent. Today he broke with sadness, now a thing inured, with the dread of the accepted. Earth had warped his belief, earth, with its somewhat limited pace, with its saffron-hued imagining, its attrition rifted with the acts of monsters. No one would have to forget him, for self-interest had never aided him, had never sketched him whole for another's gaze. Across the whitewashed ceiling of his room, birds had passed, but their flash had melted into his sleep.

The veil of the lunar landscape, now lifted high, unfolds its aromatic colors above this personage of whom I speak. He comes forth lit by the cold and forever turns his back on the springtime never there.

[MAC]

LE REQUIN ET LA MOUETTE

Je vois enfin la mer dans sa triple harmonie, la mer qui tranche de son croissant la dynastie des douleurs absurdes, la grande volière sauvage, la mer crédule comme un liseron.

Quand je dis: *j'ai levé la loi, j'ai franchi la morale, j'ai maillé le cœur*, ce n'est pas pour me donner raison devant ce pèse-néant dont la rumeur étend sa palme au delà de ma persuasion. Mais rien de ce qui m'a vu vivre et agir jusqu'ici n'est témoin alentour. Mon épaule peut bien sommeiller, ma jeunesse accourir. C'est de cela seul qu'il faut tirer richesse immédiate et opérante. Ainsi, il y a un jour de pur dans l'année, un jour qui creuse sa galerie merveilleuse dans l'écume de la mer, un jour qui monte aux yeux pour couronner midi. Hier la noblesse était déserte, le rameau était distant de ses bourgeons. Le requin et la mouette ne communiquaient pas.

Ô Vous, arc-en-ciel de ce rivage polisseur, approchez le navire de son espérance. Faites que toute fin supposée soit une neuve innocence, un fiévreux en-avant pour ceux qui trébuchent dans la matinale lourdeur.

SUZERAIN

Nous commençons toujours notre vie sur un crépuscule admirable. Tout ce qui nous aidera, plus tard, à nous dégager de nos déconvenues s'assemble autour de nos premiers pas.

La conduite des hommes de mon enfance avait l'apparence d'un sourire du ciel adressé à la charité terrestre. On y saluait le mal comme une incartade du soir. Le passage d'un météore attendrissait. Je me rends compte que l'enfant que je fus, prompt à s'éprendre comme à se blesser, a eu beaucoup de chance. J'ai marché sur le miroir d'une rivière pleine d'anneaux de couleuvre et de danses de papillons. J'ai joué dans des vergers dont la robuste vieillesse donnait des fruits. Je me suis tapi dans des roseaux, sous la garde d'êtres forts comme des chênes et sensibles comme des oiseaux.

THE SHARK AND THE GULL

At last I can see the sea in its triple harmony: the sea whose crescent blade cuts off the dynasty of absurd griefs, the great wild bird-preserve, and the sea as credulous as a bindweed.

When I say: *I have lifted the law, I am beyond morality, I have armored my heart,* it is not to justify myself before that void-meter, whose rumor extends its palm branch beyond my persuasion. But nothing of all that which has watched me live and act surrounds me now as witness. My shoulder may well doze, and my youth come running. From that alone must any immediate and effective wealth be drawn. Thus, one day out of the year is pure, a day that digs its mine of wonders in the sea-foam, a day that ascends to the eyes, crowning noon. Yesterday, nobility was a desert, the branch was remote from its buds. The shark and the gull could not communicate.

O rainbow of this gem-cutting shore, bring the ship nearer to its longing. Let every supposed end be a new innocence, a feverish forward march to those stumbling in morning torpor.   [JM]

LORD

We always begin our lives in a wonderful twilight. All that will later help to rescue us from our failure gathers about our first steps.

The behavior of men in my childhood was like the sky smiling on earth's charity. Evil was treated as a prank of evening. The fall of a meteor moved us to tenderness. I realize that the child I was, quick to love and quick to be hurt, was very lucky. I walked on the mirror of a river of coiling snakes and dancing butterflies. I played in orchards that in their robust old age were giving fruit. I hid among reeds under the care of creatures strong as oaks and sensitive as birds.

Ce monde net est mort sans laisser de charnier. Il n'est plus resté que souches calcinées, surfaces errantes, informe pugilat et l'eau bleue d'un puits minuscule veillée par cet Ami silencieux. La connaissance eut tôt fait de grandir entre nous. *Ceci n'est plus*, avais-je coutume de dire. *Ceci n'est pas*, corrigeait-il. *Pas* et *plus* étaient disjoints. Il m'offrait, à la gueule d'un serpent qui souriait, mon impossible que je pénétrais sans souffrir. D'où venait cet Ami? Sans doute, du moins sombre, du moins ouvrier des soleils. Son énergie que je jugeais grande éclatait en fougères patientes, humidité pour mon espoir. Ce dernier, en vérité, n'était qu'une neige de l'existence, l'affinité du renouveau. Un butin s'amoncelait, dessinant le littoral cruel que j'aurais un jour à parcourir. Le cœur de mon Ami m'entrait dans le cœur comme un trident, cœur souverain égaillé dans des conquêtes bientôt réduites en cendres, pour marquer combien la tentation se déprime chez qui s'établit, se rend. Nos confidences ne construiraient pas d'église; le mutisme reconduisait tous nos pouvoirs.

Il m'apprit à voler au-dessus de la nuit des mots, loin de l'hébétude des navires à l'ancre. Ce n'est pas le glacier qui nous importe mais ce qui le fait possible indéfiniment, sa solitaire vraisemblance. Je nouai avec des haines enthousiastes que j'aidai à vaincre puis quittai. (Il suffit de fermer les yeux pour ne plus être reconnu). Je retirai aux choses l'illusion qu'elles produisent pour se préserver de nous et leur laissai la part qu'elle nous concède. Je vis qu'il n'y aurait jamais de femme pour moi dans MA ville. La frenésie des cascades, symboliquement, acquitterait mon bon vouloir.

J'ai remonté ainsi l'âge de la solitude jusqu'à la demeure suivante de l'HOMME VIOLET. Mais il ne disposait là que du morose état-civil de ses prisons, de son expérience muette de persécuté, et nous n'avions, nous, que son signalement d'évadé.

That flawless world is dead, and has left no bones. Nothing but burnt stumps, drifting surfaces, formless fight, and the blue water of a tiny well, guarded by my silent Friend.

Understanding grew up between us very soon. *That no longer exists,* I used to say. *That does not exist,* he would correct me. *Not* and *no longer* were disjoined. He showed me my impossibility in the jaws of a smiling serpent, and I entered without anguish. Where did my Friend come from? No doubt from the least dim, least laboring of suns. His energy, which I took to be great, burst out in patient ferns to water my hope. The latter, in truth, was only a snow of existence, an affinity of spring. Booty was piling up, lining the cruel shore which I should one day have to cross. My Friend's heart pierced my heart like a trident—a king's heart dissipated in conquests that soon fell to ashes, showing how temptation loses face in anyone who settles and surrenders. Our secrets would not build a church; muteness drained away all our powers.

He taught me to fly above the night of words, far above the apathy of ships at anchor. It is not the glacier that matters, but that which makes it possible indefinitely, its solitary plausibility. I joined with several enthusiastic hatreds, helped them to win, then left them. (All I had to do, not to be recognized, was close my eyes.) I stripped from things the illusion they create for protection against us, and left them the part they yield to us. I saw that there would never be a woman for me in MY city. The frenzy of cascades would, symbolically, carry out my good intentions.

Thus, I went back through the age of solitude to the next dwelling of VIOLET MAN. But there, all he had was the morose list of the prisons he had served in, certifying to his mute experience of persecution, and all *we* had was the description of him as an escapee. [JM]

LE MÉTÉORE DU 13 AOÛT

(Le Météore du 13 août)

À la seconde où tu m'apparus, mon coeur eut tout le ciel pour l'éclairer. Il fut midi à mon poème. Je sus que l'angoisse dormait.

(Novae)

Premier rayon qui hésite entre l'imprécation du supplice et le magnifique amour.

L'optimisme des philosophies ne nous est plus suffisant.

La lumière du rocher abrite un arbre majeur. Nous nous avançons vers sa visibilité.

Toujours plus larges fiançailles des regards. La tragédie qui s'élabore jouira même de nos limites.

Le danger nous ôtait toute mélancolie. Nous parlions sans nous regarder. Le temps nous tenait unis. La mort nous évitait.

Alouettes de la nuit, étoiles, qui tournoyez aux sources de l'abandon, soyez progrès aux fronts qui dorment.

J'ai sauté de mon lit bordé d'aubépines. Pieds nus, je parle aux enfants.

(La lune change de jardin)

Où vais-je égarer cette fortune d'excréments qui m'escorte comme une lampe?

Hymnes provisoires! hymnes contredits!

Folles, et, à la nuit, lumières obéissantes.

Orageuse liberté dans les langes de la foudre, sur la souveraineté du vide, aux petites mains de l'homme.

Ne t'étourdis pas de lendemains. Tu regardes l'hiver qui enjambe les plaies et ronge les fenêtres, et, sur le porche de la mort, l'inscrutable torture.

THE METEOR OF AUGUST 13TH

(The Meteor of August 13th)

The second you appeared to me, my heart had all the sky to light its way. It was my poem's noon. I knew that anguish slept.

(Novae)

First ray which hesitates between the imprecation of agony and a magnificent love.

Philosophy's optimism is no longer enough.

The rock's light shelters a major tree. We go forward toward its visibility.

Ever deeper wedding of the eyes. The tragedy now unfolding will delight even in our limits.

Danger did away with all our melancholy. We talked without looking at each other. Time held us together. Death avoided us.

Larks of the night, stars, whirling at the wellsprings of abandon, be progress to the brows that sleep.

I have leapt from my hawthorn-bordered bed. Barefoot, I talk to children.

(The Moon Changes Gardens)

Where shall I scatter this treasure of excrement which escorts me like a lamp?

Provisional hymns! Hymns contradicted!

Demented lights, obedient to the night.

Stormy freedom swaddled in lightning, above the sovereignty of the void, in the small hands of man.

Do not lose yourself in tomorrows. You watch winter striding over wounds, gnawing at windows, and, on death's porch, inscrutable torture.

Ceux qui dorment dans la laine, ceux qui courent dans le froid, ceux qui offrent leur médiation, ceux qui ne sont pas ravisseurs faute de mieux, s'accordent avec le météore, ennemi du coq.

Illusoirement, je suis à la fois dans mon âme et hors d'elle, loin devant la vitre et contre la vitre, saxifrage éclaté. Ma convoitise est infinie. Rien ne m'obsède que la vie.

Étincelle nomade qui meurt dans son incendie.

Aime riveraine. Dépense ta vérité. L'herbe qui cache l'or de ton amour ne connaîtra jamais le gel.

Sur cette terre des périls, je m'émerveille de l'idolâtrie de la vie.

Que ma présence qui vous cause énigmatique malaise, haine sans rémission, soit météore dans votre âme.

Un chant d'oiseau surprend la branche du matin.

LES PREMIERS INSTANTS

Nous regardions couler devant nous l'eau grandissante. Elle effaçait d'un coup la montagne, se chassant de ses flancs maternels. Ce n'était pas un torrent qui s'offrait à son destin mais une bête ineffable dont nous devenions la parole et la substance. Elle nous tenait amoureux sur l'arc tout-puissant de son imagination. Quelle intervention eût pu nous contraindre? La modicité quotidienne avait fui, le sang jeté était rendu à sa chaleur. Adoptés par l'ouvert, poncés jusqu'à l'invisible, nous étions une victoire qui ne prendrait jamais fin.

Those who sleep in wool, who run in the cold, who offer their mediation, who are not predators for want of better, are in phase with the meteor, enemy of the cock.

Illusorily, I am both in my soul and outside it, far in front of the windowpane and pressed up against the windowpane, a split saxifrage. My lust is infinite. Nothing obsesses me but life.

A nomad spark dying in its fire.

Love a river girl. Spend your truth. The grass which hides your love's gold will never know frost.

On this perilous earth, I marvel at life's idolatry.

May my presence, which causes you enigmatic uneasiness, unremitting hatred, be a meteor in your soul.

A birdsong surprises the morning's branch.   [NK]

THE FIRST MOMENTS

We were watching the water as it flowed, increasing before us. It effaced the mountain suddenly, expelling itself from her maternal side. Not a torrent submitting to its fate but an ineffable beast whose word and substance we became. It held us amorous on the all-powerful arch of its imagination. What intervention could have constrained us? Daily tameness had fled, blood cast aside was rendered to its heat. Adopted by the open, abraded to invisibility, we were a victory that would never end.

[MAC]

FASTES

L'été chantait sur son roc préféré quand tu m'es apparue, l'été chantait à l'écart de nous qui étions silence, sympathie, liberté triste, mer plus encore que la mer dont la longue pelle bleue s'amusait à nos pieds. L'été chantait et ton cœur nageait loin de lui. Je baisais ton courage, entendais ton désarroi. Route par l'absolu des vagues vers ces hauts pics d'écume où croisent des vertus meurtrières pour les mains qui portent nos maisons. Nous n'étions pas crédules. Nous étions entourés. Les ans passèrent. Les orages moururent. Le monde s'en alla. J'avais mal de sentir que ton cœur justement ne m'apercevait plus. Je t'aimais. En mon absence de visage et mon vide de bonheur. Je t'aimais, changeant en tout, fidèle à toi.

LA SORGUE

Chanson pour Yvonne

Rivière trop tôt partie, d'une traite, sans compagnon,
Donne aux enfants de mon pays le visage de ta passion.

Rivière où l'éclair finit et où commence ma maison,
Qui roule aux marches d'oubli la rocaille de ma raison.

Rivière, en toi terre est frisson, soleil anxiété.
Que chaque pauvre dans sa nuit fasse son pain de ta moisson.

Rivère souvent punie, rivière à l'abandon.

Rivière des apprentis à la calleuse condition,
Il n'est vent qui ne fléchisse à la crête de tes sillons.

Rivière de l'âme vide, de la guenille et du soupçon,
Du vieux malheur qui se dévide, de l'ormeau, de la compassion.

Rivière des farfelus, des fiévreux, des équarrisseurs,
Du soleil lâchant sa charrue pour s'acoquiner au menteur.

ANNALS

Summer was singing on its favorite rock when you appeared to me, summer was singing apart as we who were silence, sympathy, sorrowful freedom, were sea still more than the sea whose long blue spade was playing at our feet.

Summer was singing and your heart swam far from it. I embraced your courage, heard your confusion. Road along the absolute of waves toward those high peaks of foam where virtues sail, murderous to hands bearing our houses. We were not credulous. We were surrounded.

The years passed by. The storms died down. The world went its way. I suffered to think it was your heart which no longer perceived me. I loved you. In my absence of visage and my emptiness of joy. I loved you, changing in every way, faithful to you.   [MAC]

THE SORGUE

Song for Yvonne

River setting out without companion, too soon, at a bound,
Give the children of my country the face of your passion.

River where the lightning ends and my home begins,
That rolls the rubble of my reason down the frontiers of forgetfulness.

River, in you the earth quivers, the sun is uneasy,
Let every poor man harvest your bread in his night.

River often punished, often left alone.

River of the apprentices to our calloused condition,
There is no wind which does not bend to the crest of your wake.

River of the empty soul, of rags and of suspicion,
Of old misfortunes unwinding, of elm trees, of compassion.

River of the hare-brained, of the feverish, of flayers,
Of the sun leaving its plough to sink to the level of lies.

Rivière des meilleurs que soi, rivière des brouillards éclos,
De la lampe qui désaltère l'angoisse autour de son chapeau.

Rivière des égards au songe, rivière qui rouille le fer,
Où les étoiles ont cette ombre qu'elles refusent à la mer.

Rivière des pouvoirs transmis et du cri embouquant les eaux,
De l'ouragan qui mord la vigne et annonce le vin nouveau.

Rivière au cœur jamais détruit dans ce monde fou de prison,
Garde-nous violent et ami des abeilles de l'horizon.

LE MARTINET

Martinet aux ailes trop larges, qui vire et crie sa joie autour de la maison.
Tel est le cœur.

Il dessèche le tonnerre. Il sème dans le ciel serein. S'il touche au sol, il se déchire.

Sa repartie est l'hirondelle. Il déteste la familière. Que vaut dentelle de la tour?

Sa pause est au creux le plus sombre. Nul n'est plus à l'étroit que lui.

L'été de la longue clarté, il filera dans les ténèbres, par les persiennes de minuit.

Il n'est pas d'yeux pour le tenir. Il crie, c'est toute sa présence. Un mince fusil va l'abattre. Tel est le cœur.

River of one's betters, river of the clear fog,
Of the lamp which freezes the fear around its shade.

River of regard for dreams, river that rusts iron,
Where the stars keep the shadow they hold back from the sea.

River of powers yielded, of cries entering its watery mouth,
Of the hurricane that gnaws the grape and announces the new wine.

River with an indestructible heart in this mad prison-world,
Keep us violent and friends to the bees on the horizon.   [MR]

THE SWIFT

Swift with wings too wide, wheeling and shrieking his joy as he circles the house. Such is the heart.

He dries up thunder. He sows in the serene sky. If he touches ground, he tears himself apart.

His response is the swallow, the familiar, whom he detests. What value has lace from the tower?

His pause is in the most somber hollow. No one lives in space more narrow than he.

Through the summer of long brightness, he will streak his way in shadows, by the blinds of midnight.

No eyes can hold him. He shrieks for his only presence. A slight gun is about to fell him. Such is the heart.   [MAC]

MADELEINE À LA VEILLEUSE

par Georges de La Tour

Je voudrais aujourd'hui que l'herbe fût blanche pour fouler l'évidence de vous voir souffrir: je ne regarderais pas sous votre main si jeune la forme dure, sans crépi de la mort. Un jour discrétionnaire, d'autres pourtant moins avides que moi, retireront votre chemise de toile, occuperont votre alcôve. Mais ils oublieront en partant de noyer la veilleuse et un peu d'huile se répandra par le poignard de la flamme sur l'impossible solution.

MADELEINE QUI VEILLAIT

27 janvier 1948

J'ai dîné chez mon ami le peintre Jean Villeri. Il est plus de onze heures. Le métro me ramène à mon domicile. Je change de rame à la station Trocadéro. Alourdi par une fatigue agréable, j'écoute distraitement résonner mon pas dans le couloir des correspondances. Soudain une jeune femme, qui vient en sens inverse, m'aborde après m'avoir, je crois, longuement dévisagé. Elle m'adresse une demande pour le moins inattendue: "Vous n'auriez pas une feuille de papier à lettres, monsieur?" Sur ma réponse négative et sans doute devant mon air amusé, elle ajoute: "Cela vous paraît drôle?" Je réponds non, bien sûr, ce propos ou un autre . . . Elle prononce avec une nuance de regret: "Pourtant!" Sa maigreur, sa pâleur et l'éclat de ses yeux sont extrêmes. Elle marche avec cette aisance des mauvais métiers qui est aussi la mienne. Je cherche en vain à cette silhouette fâcheuse quelque beauté. Il est certain que l'ovale du visage, le front, le regard surtout doivent retenir l'attention, troubler. Mais de là à s'enquérir! Je ne songe qu'à fausser compagnie. Je suis arrivé devant la rame de Saint-Cloud et je monte rapidement. Elle s'élance derrière moi. Je fais quelques pas dans le wagon pour m'éloigner et rompre. Sans résultat. A Michel-Ange-Molitor je m'empresse de descendre. Mais le léger pas me poursuit et me rattrape. Le timbre de la voix s'est modifié. Un ton de prière sans humilité. En quelques mots paisibles je précise que les choses doivent en rester là. Elle dit alors: "Vous ne comprenez pas, oh non! Ce n'est pas ce que vous croyez." L'air de la nuit que nous atteignons donne de la grâce à son effronterie: "Me voyez-vous dans les couloirs déserts d'une station, que les gens sont pressés de quitter, proposer la galante aventure?—Où habitez-vous?—Très loin d'ici. Vous ne con-

MADELEINE WITH THE VIGIL-LAMP
by Georges de La Tour

I would wish today that the grass were white to trample the visible signs of your suffering: I'd not look under your hand, so young, at death's hard form without rough-cast. One discretionary day, others, though less avid than I, will remove your rough linen blouse, will occupy your alcove. But they will forget to extinguish the lamp in their departing and a little oil will spill out by the dagger of the flame onto the impossible solution. [MAC]

MAGDALENE WAITING

27 January 1948

I've just come from supper with a friend, the painter Jean Villeri. It is past eleven. The *métro* is taking me home. At the Trocadero I change cars. Heavy with an agreeable lassitude, I listen casually to the sound of my own footsteps in the connecting passageway. Suddenly a young woman coming from the opposite direction accosts me, after, I think, for a long time watching me from a distance. "You wouldn't have a piece of writing paper about you, sir?" At my answer in the negative and doubtless from my air of amusement, she adds, "That seems funny to you." I said, no, not at all, one approach or another . . . Then with a touch of sadness: "Well!" Her thinness, her pallor and the brilliance of her eyes are beyond the ordinary. She walks with that relaxed air of the underworld which is as well my own. I seek without success in that pitiful silhouette some beauty. Surely the oval of the face, her forehead, the look in her eyes should hold the attention, rouse some interest. However, I seek only to avoid her. I come to the platform for St. Cloud and step quickly into the train. She clambers in behind me. I walk through the car to get away from her. No use. At Michel-Ange-Molitor I hasten to get off. But the light step follows and overtakes me. The tone of the voice has changed. A pleading without humility. In a few quiet words I explain that things must stop here. Then she said: "You don't understand. Oh no! It is not what you think." The night air lent a certain grace to her effrontery. "You find me here, as you think, in the corridors of a subway station which the crowd has just hurried to leave, proposing *galante* adventures?" "Where do you live?" "Far from here. You wouldn't know." The memory of my early pursuit of enigmas, in the time of my discovery of life and of poetry, returns

naissez pas." Le souvenir de la quête des énigmes, au temps de ma découverte de la vie et de la poésie, me revient à l'esprit. Je le chasse, agacé. "Je ne suis pas tenté par l'impossible comme autrefois (je mens). J'ai trop vu souffrir . . . (quelle indécence!)" Et sa réponse: "Croire à nouveau ne fait pas qu'il y aura davantage de souffrance. Restez accueillant. Vous ne vous verrez pas mourir." Elle sourit: "Comme la nuit est humide!" Je la sens ainsi. La rue Boileau, d'habitude provinciale et rassurante, est blanche de gelée, mais je cherche en vain la trace des étoiles dans le ciel. J'observe de biais la jeune femme: "Comment vous appelez-vous, mon petit?—Madeleine." A vrai dire, son nom ne m'a pas surpris. J'ai terminé dans l'après-midi *Madeleine à la veilleuse,* inspiré par le tableau de Georges de La Tour dont l'interrogation est si actuelle. Ce poème m'a coûté. Comment ne pas entrevoir, dans cette passante opiniâtre, sa vérification? A deux reprises déjà, pour d'autres particulièrement coûteux poèmes, la même aventure m'advint. Je n'ai nulle difficulté à m'en convaincre. L'accès d'une couche profonde d'émotion et de vision est propice au surgissement du grand réel. On ne l'atteint pas sans quelque remerciement de l'oracle. Je ne pense pas qu'il soit absurde de l'affirmer. Je ne suis pas le seul à qui ces rares preuves sont parfois foncièrement accordées. "Madeleine, vous avez été très bonne et très patiente. Allons ensemble, encore, voulez-vous?" Nous marchons dans une intelligence d'ombres parfaite. J'ai pris le bras de la jeune femme et j'éprouve ces similitudes que la sensation de la maigreur éveille. Elles disparaissent presque aussitôt, ne laissant place qu'à l'intense solitude et à la complète faveur à la fois, que je ressentis quand j'eus mis le point final à l'écriture de mon poème. Il est minuit et demi. Avenue de Versailles, la lumière du métro Javel, pâle, monte de terre. "Je vous dis adieu, ici." J'hésite, mais le frêle corps se libère. "Embrassez-moi, que je parte heureuse . . ." Je prends sa tête dans mes mains et la baise aux yeux et sur les cheveux. Madeleine s'en va, s'efface au bas des marches de l'escalier du métro dont les portes de fer vont être bientôt tirées et sont déjà prêtes.

Je jure que tout ceci est vrai et m'est arrivé, n'étant pas sans amour, comme j'en fais le récit, cette nuit de janvier.

La réalité noble ne se dérobe pas à qui la rencontre pour l'estimer et non pour l'insulter ou la faire prisonnière. Là est l'unique condition que nous ne sommes pas toujours assez purs pour remplir.

to my mind. Annoyed, I banish the thought at once. "I am not tempted (I lie) by the impossible as I was formerly. I have seen too much suffering (how indecent)." And her answer: "To believe anew will not increase the suffering. Be open. You will not look upon your own death." She sighs: "How damp the night is!" I felt it too. Rue Boileau, usually provincial and reassuring, is white with frost, but I search vainly for any trace of stars. I glance from the corner of my eye at the young woman: "What's your name, my child?" "Magdalene." To tell the truth, her name did not surprise me. I had finished writing that very afternoon *Mary Magdalene Sitting by Lamplight,* inspired by the painting of Georges de La Tour, in which the questioning is so actual. That poem cost me heavily. How should I not recognize in this persistent passer-by just the verification I sought? Already on two occasions, by grace of particularly costly poems, the same thing had happened to me. I have no difficulty whatever in convincing myself. A profound birth of emotion and vision propitious to the welling up of the enormous Real. One does not attain it save with the consent of the oracle. I do not think it is absurd to affirm this. I am not the only one to whom from time to time these deep-seated proofs are accorded. "Magdalene, you have been very patient and very good. Let's walk on together awhile, shall we?" We went on walking in that perfect intelligence of the darkness. I took the young woman's arm and experienced that feeling which a sense of extreme emaciation awakes in one. It vanished almost at once, leaving only an intense emptiness and, at the same time, the sense of complete reward I felt when I had put the final dot to my poem. It is half an hour after midnight. Avenue de Versailles, the pale light of the Javel *métro* station rises from the ground. "Here I tell you good-bye." I hesitate but the frail body has already freed itself from my grip. "Kiss me, so I may depart happy. . . ." I take her head in my hands and press my lips to her eyes, her hair. It is the surface of a field moistened by evening dew. Magdalene is gone, swallowed by the stairway of the *métro,* of which the iron doors are ajar and will soon be closed.

I swear all this is true and happened to me, not without love, as I have recounted it, this January night.

Reality, noble, does not refuse herself to the one who comes to prize her, not to insult or take her prisoner. There lies the unique condition we are not always pure enough to supply. [WCW]

63

ALLÉGEANCE

Dans les rues de la ville il y a mon amour. Peu importe où il va dans le temps divisé. Il n'est plus mon amour, chacun peut lui parler. Il ne se souvient plus; qui au juste l'aima?

Il cherche son pareil dans le vœu des regards. L'espace qu'il parcourt est ma fidélité. Il dessine l'espoir et léger l'éconduit. Il est prépondérant sans qu'il y prenne part.

Je vis au fond de lui comme une épave heureuse. A son insu, ma solitude est son trésor. Dans le grand méridien où s'inscrit son essor, ma liberté le creuse.

Dans les rues de la ville il y a mon amour. Peu importe où il va dans le temps divisé. Il n'est plus mon amour, chacun peut lui parler. Il ne se souvient plus; qui au juste l'aima et l'éclaire de loin pour qu'il ne tombe pas?

ALLEGIANCE

In the streets of the town goes my love. Small matter where she moves in divided time. She is no longer my love, anyone may speak with her. She remembers no longer: who exactly loved her?

She seeks her equal in glances, pledging. The space she traverses is my faithfulness. She traces a hope and lightly dismisses it. She is dominant without taking part.

I live in her depth, a joyous shipwreck. Without her knowing, my solitude is her treasure. In the great meridian where her soaring is inscribed, my freedom delves deep in her.

In the streets of the town goes my love. Small matter where she moves in divided time. She is no longer my love, anyone may speak with her. She remembers no longer: who exactly loved her, and lights her from afar, lest she should fall?   [MAC]

Les Matinaux

QU'IL VIVE!

Ce pays n'est qu'un vœu de l'esprit, un contre-sépulcre.

Dans mon pays, les tendres preuves du printemps et les oiseaux mal habillés sont préférés aux buts lointains.

La vérité attend l'aurore à côté d'une bougie. Le verre de fenêtre est négligé. Qu'importe à l'attentif.

Dans mon pays, on ne questionne pas un homme ému.

Il n'y a pas d'ombre maligne sur la barque chavirée.

Bonjour à peine, est inconnu dans mon pays.

On n'emprunte que ce qui peut se rendre augmenté.

Il y a des feuilles, beaucoup de feuilles sur les arbres de mon pays. Les branches sont libres de n'avoir pas de fruits.

On ne croit pas à la bonne foi du vainqueur.

Dans mon pays, on remercie.

The Dawn Breakers

LONG LIVE . . .

> *This country is but a wish of the spirit, a counter-sepulcher.*

In my country, tender proofs of spring and badly dressed birds are preferred to far-off goals.

Truth waits for dawn beside a candle. Window glass is neglected. To the watchful, what does it matter?

In my country, we don't question a man deeply moved.

There is no malignant shadow on the capsized boat.

A cool hello is unknown in my country.

We borrow only what can be returned increased.

There are leaves, many leaves, on the trees of my country. The branches are free to bear no fruits.

We don't believe in the good faith of the victor.

In my country, we say thank you.   [MAC]

67

LE TOUT ENSEMBLE

Faucille qui persévérez dans le ciel désuni
Malgré le jour et notre frénésie.
Lune qui nous franchis et côtoies notre cœur,
Lui, resté dans la nuit.
Liens que rien n'interrompt
Sous le talon actif, par les midis glacés.

Déjà là, printanier crépuscule!
Nous n'étions qu'éveillés, nous n'avons pas agi.

LE CARREAU

Pures pluies, femmes attendues,
La face que vous essuyez,
De verre voué aux tourments,
Est la face du révolté;
L'autre, la vitre de l'heureux,
Frissonne devant le feu de bois.

Je vous aime mystères jumeaux,
Je touche à chacun de vous;
J'ai mal et je suis léger.

THE ASSEMBLED WHOLE

Sickle maintained in the disordered heavens
Even in the midst of morning and our frenzy.
Moon which goes beyond us to skirt the edges of the heart,
The heart remaining in darkness.
Bonds which nothing can break
Under the active heel, through chilling noons.

Already here, O vernal twilight!
We were awake, but have not stirred.   [WJS]

THE WINDOWPANE

Pure rains, awaited women,
The face you bathe,
Of glass doomed to torment,
Is the face of the rebel;
The other, the happy windowpane,
Shivers before the wood fire.

I love you, twin mysteries,
I touch upon each of you;
I hurt and I am weightless.   [NK]

L'AMOUREUSE EN SECRET

Elle a mis le couvert et mené à la perfection ce à quoi son amour assis en face d'elle parlera bas tout à l'heure, en la dévisageant. Cette nourriture semblable à l'anche d'un hautbois.

Sous la table, ses chevilles nues caressent à présent la chaleur du bien-aimé, tandis que des voix qu'elle n'entend pas, la complimentent. Le rayon de la lampe emmêle, tisse sa distraction sensuelle.

Un lit, très loin, sait-elle, patiente et tremble dans l'exil des draps odorants, comme un lac de montagne qui ne sera jamais abandonné.

L'ADOLESCENT SOUFFLETÉ

Les mêmes coups qui l'envoyaient au sol le lançaient en même temps loin devant sa vie, vers les futures années où, quand il saignerait, ce ne serait plus à cause de l'iniquité d'un seul. Tel l'arbuste que réconfortent ses racines et qui presse ses rameaux meurtris contre son fût résistant, il descendait ensuite à reculons dans le mutisme de ce savoir et dans son innocence. Enfin il s'échappait, s'enfuyait et devenait souverainement heureux. Il atteignait la prairie et la barrière des roseaux dont il cajolait la vase et percevait le sec frémissement. Il semblait que ce que la terre avait produit de plus noble et de plus persévérant, l'avait, en compensation, adopté.

Il recommencerait ainsi jusqu'au moment où, la nécessité de rompre disparue, il se tiendrait droit et attentif parmi les hommes, à la fois plus vulnérable et plus fort.

THE GIRL SECRETLY IN LOVE

She has set the table, and brought to perfection in her mind what her lover, seated opposite her, will answer softly in a little while, looking in her face. This food is like the reed of an oboe.

Under the table now, her naked ankles caress her lover's warmth, while voices which she does not hear, compliment her. The beam of the lamp tangles, weaves her voluptuous distraction.

Far away a bed lies patient and trembling in the exile of its fragrant covers, like a mountain lake that will never be abandoned.   [JW]

THE ADOLESCENT CHASTISED

The same blows that cast him to the ground projected him at once far ahead into his life, toward the future years when, wounded, he would no longer bleed from the iniquity of one being. Like the bush solaced by its roots, pressing its bruised boughs against its resistant bole, he would then descend backward into the silence of this knowledge and into its innocence. At last he escaped fleeing, and attained a sovereign happiness. He reached the meadow and the barrier of reeds whose slime he coaxed and whose dry quivering he watched. It seemed that the noblest and most enduring things that the earth had brought forth had, in compensation, adopted him.

Thus he would start again until, no longer needing to break off the battle, he could hold himself upright and attentive among men, more vulnerable and yet stronger.   [MAC]

ANOUKIS ET PLUS TARD JEANNE

Je te découvrirai à ceux que j'aime, comme un long éclair de chaleur, aussi inexplicablement que tu t'es montrée à moi, Jeanne, quand, un matin s'astreignant à ton dessein, tu nous menas de roc en roc jusqu'à cette fin de soi qu'on appelle un sommet. Le visage à demi masqué par ton bras replié, les doigts de ta main sollicitant ton épaule, tu nous offris, au terme de notre ascension, une ville, les souffrances et la qualification d'un génie, la surface égarée d'un désert, et le tournant circonspect d'un fleuve sur la rive duquel des bâtisseurs s'interrogeaient. Mais je te suis vite revenu, Faucille, car tu consumais ton offrande. Et ni le temps, ni la beauté, ni le hasard qui débride le coeur ne pouvaient se mesurer avec toi.

J'ai ressuscité alors mon antique richesse, notre richesse à tous, et dominant ce que demain détruira, je me suis souvenu que tu étais Anoukis l'Étreigneuse, aussi fantastiquement que tu étais Jeanne, la soeur de mon meilleur ami, et aussi inexplicablement que tu étais l'Étrangère dans l'esprit de ce misérable carillonneur dont le père répétait autrefois que Van Gogh était fou.

LES LICHENS

Je marchais parmi les bosses d'une terre écurée, les haleines secrètes, les plantes sans mémoire. La montagne se levait, flacon empli d'ombre qu'étreignait par instant le geste de la soif. Ma trace, mon existence se perdaient. Ton visage glissait à reculons devant moi. Ce n'était qu'une tache à la recherche de l'abeille qui la ferait fleur et la dirait vivante. Nous allions nous séparer. Tu demeurerais sur le plateau des arômes et je pénétrerais dans le jardin du vide. Là, sous la sauvegarde des rochers, dans la plénitude du vent, je demanderais à la nuit véritable de disposer de mon sommeil pour accroître ton bonheur. Et tous les fruits t'appartiendraient.

ANOUKIS AND LATER JEANNE

I will unveil you to those I love, like a long stroke of summer lightning, as inexplicably as you showed yourself to me, Jeanne, on a morning made to your design when you led us from rock to rock up to that end of self we call a summit. Your face half-masked by the arm you bent, the fingers of your hand seeking your shoulder, you offered us at the end of our ascent a city, the sufferings and qualifications of a genius, the scattered surface of a desert, and the circumspect turning of a river, on whose bank some builders stood questioning. But quickly I came back to you, my Reaper, for you were consuming your offering. And neither time nor beauty nor chance which unbridles the heart could compare with you.

It was then I revived my ancient wealth, the wealth of all of us, and dominating what tomorrow will destroy, I remembered you were Anoukis the Clasper, just as incredibly as you were Jeanne, my best friend's sister, and as inexplicably as you were the Foreigner to that miserable bellringer whose father always used to say Van Gogh was crazy.   [NK]

THE LICHENS

I walked among the hummocks of a land scoured, the secret breaths, the plants without memory. The mountain rose up, a shadow-filled flask embraced now and again by the gesture of thirst. My track, my existence were slowly fading. Your face slipped away retreating in front of me. It was only a spot in search of the bee that would make of it a flower and call it alive. We were going to separate. You would remain on the high plain of scents and I would enter the garden of the void. There, in the safekeeping of rocks, in the wind's fullness, I would place my sleep at the disposition of the true night for it to deepen your happiness. And all the fruits would be yours by right.   [MAC]

LES INVENTEURS

Ils sont venus, les forestiers de l'autre versant, les inconnus de nous, les
  rebelles à nos usages.
Ils sont venus nombreux.
Leur troupe est apparue à la ligne de partage des cèdres
Et du champ de la vieille moisson désormais irrigué et vert.
La longue marche les avait échauffés.
Leur casquette cassait sur leurs yeux et leur pied fourbu se posait dans le
  vague.
Ils nous ont aperçus et se sont arrêtés.
Visiblement ils ne présumaient pas nous trouver là,
Sur des terres faciles et des sillons bien clos,
Tout à fait insouciants d'une audience.
Nous avons levé le front et les avons encouragés.

Le plus disert s'est approché, puis un second tout aussi déraciné et lent.
Nous sommes venus, dirent-ils, vous prévenir de l'arrivée prochaine de
  l'ouragan, de votre implacable adversaire.
Pas plus que vous, nous ne le connaissons
Autrement que par des relations et des confidences d'ancêtres.
Mais pourquoi sommes-nous heureux incompréhensiblement devant vous et
  soudain pareils à des enfants?

Nous avons dit merci et les avons congédiés.
Mais auparavant ils ont bu, et leurs mains tremblaient, et leurs yeux riaient
  sur les bords.
Hommes d'arbres et de cognée, capables de tenir tête à quelque terreur, mais
  inaptes à conduire l'eau, à aligner des bâtisses, à les enduire de couleurs
  plaisantes,
Ils ignoreraient le jardin d'hiver et l'économie de la joie.

Certes, nous aurions pu les convaincre et les conquérir,
Car l'angoisse de l'ouragan est émouvante.
Oui, l'ouragan allait bientôt venir;
Mais cela valait-il la peine que l'on en parlât et qu'on dérangeât l'avenir?
Là où nous sommes, il n'y a pas de crainte urgente.

THE INVENTORS

They came, the foresters from the other side, the unknown to us, the hostile
    to our ways.
They came, and they were many.
Their host appeared at the line dividing the cedar woods
From a field long harvested that even now rose fresh and green.
The long march had warmed them.
Their caps broke over their eyes and their tired feet foundered somewhere
    distant.
They caught sight of us and halted.
Clearly they had not thought to find us there,
On a land where the soil was easy and the furrow close,
Quite heedless of an audience.
We raised out heads and beckoned them to come on.

The most fluent among them came over, then a second, likewise rootless and
    slow.
We have come, they said, to warn you of the imminent arrival of the storm,
    your implacable foe.
What knowledge we have of such things, we have, as you do,
Only on hearsay and from what our ancestors have confided.
Yet why is it we feel so inexplicably happy in your presence, and so suddenly
    like children?

We thanked them and sent them once more on their way.
Yet, prior to this, they had drunk, and their hands trembled and their eyes
    laughed at the edges.
Men at home among trees and with axes, able to stand their ground before
    some terrible fear, yet unfit for the channeling of water, or the
    alignment of a building, or its coating with pleasant colors,
Of the winter garden they would know nothing, nor of the economy of joy.

Undoubtedly we could have convinced and conquered them,
For the anguish before a storm is deeply moving.
And, yes, the storm was shortly to appear.
But was that really something to be talked about and to disturb the future
    for?
At the point we have reached, there are no urgent fears.   [MH]

TOUTE VIE . . .

Toute vie qui doit poindre
achève un blessé.
Voici l'arme,
rien,
vous, moi, réversiblement
ce livre,
et l'énigme
qu'à votre tour vous deviendrez
dans le caprice amer des sables.

EVERY LIFE . . .

Every life, as it dawns,
kills one of the injured.
This is the weapon:
nothing,
you, me, interchangeably
with this book,
and the riddle
that you, too, will become
in the bitter caprice of the sands.   [JW]

Recherche de la base et du sommet

PRIÈRE ROGUE

Gardez-nous la révolte, l'éclair, l'accord illusoire, un rire pour le trophée glissé des mains, même l'entier et long fardeau qui succède, dont la difficulté nous mène à une révolte nouvelle. Gardez-nous la primevère et le destin.

A***

Tu es mon amour depuis tant d'années,
Mon vertige devant tant d'attente,
Que rien ne peut vieillir, froidir;
Même ce qui attendait notre mort,
Ou lentement sut nous combattre,
Même ce qui nous est étranger,
Et mes éclipses et mes retours.

Fermée comme un volet de buis
Une extrême chance compacte
Est notre chaîne de montagnes,
Notre comprimante splendeur.

Je dis chance, ô ma martelée;
Chacun de nous peut recevoir
La part de mystère de l'autre
Sans en répandre le secret;
Et la douleur qui vient d'ailleurs
Trouve enfin sa séparation
Dans la chair de notre unité,
Trouve enfin sa route solaire
Au centre de notre nuée
Qu'elle déchire et recommence.

Search for the Base and Summit

UNBENDING PRAYER

Preserve for us rebellion, lightning, the illusory agreement, a laugh for the trophy slipped from our hands, even the whole lengthy burden that follows, whose difficulty leads us to a new rebellion. Preserve for us fate and the primrose.   [MAC]

TO***

For years now you have been my love,
The vertigo I feel when I lie waiting
That nothing can make old, make cold;
Even that which was expecting our death,
Or gradually knew how to combat us,
Even that which we are strangers to,
My eclipses also and also my returns.

Barred like a boxwood shutter,
An extreme and compact fortune
Is our mountain range,
Our compressing splendor.

I say fortune, o my wrought one;
Each of us can receive
Another's share of mystery
Without spilling its secret;
And the suffering that comes from elsewhere
Finds at last its separation
In the flesh of our unity,
Finds at last its solar road
At the center of our dense cloud
Which it tears and recommences.

Je dis chance comme je le sens.
Tu as élevé le sommet
Que devra franchir mon attente
Quand demain disparaîtra.

I say fortune the way I feel it.
You have raised the summit
That my waiting will have to cross
When tomorrow is no longer there.   [MH]

La Parole en archipel

LASCAUX

***

II

LES CERFS NOIRS

Les eaux parlaient à l'oreille du ciel.
Cerfs, vous avez franchi l'espace millénaire,
Des ténèbres du roc aux caresses de l'air.

Le chasseur qui vous pousse, le génie qui vous voit,
Que j'aime leur passion, de mon large rivage!
Et si j'avais leurs yeux, dans l'instant où j'espère?

III

LA BÊTE INNOMMABLE

La Bête innommable ferme la marche du gracieux troupeau, comme un
cyclope bouffe.
Huit quolibets font sa parure, divisent sa folie.
La Bête rote dévotement dans l'air rustique.
Ses flancs bourrés et tombants sont douloureux, vont se vider de leur
grossesse.
De son sabot à ses vaines défenses, elle est enveloppée de fétidité.

Ainsi m'apparaît dans la frise de Lascaux, mère fantastiquement déguisée,
La Sagesse aux yeux pleins de larmes.

The Word as Archipelago

LASCAUX
* * *

II

THE BLACK STAGS

The waters were speaking into the ear of the sky.
Stags, you have leapt millennial space
From the darkness of the rock to the air's caresses.

How, from my spacious shore, I adore their passion:
The hunter who presses, and the spirit who sights you.
What if, in the instant of hope, I had their eyes?   [GS]

III

THE UNNAMEABLE BEAST

The unnameable Beast rounds off the graceful herd, like a comic cyclops.
Eight jibes adorn her and divide her folly.
The Beast belches devoutly in the country air.
Her heavy hanging flanks are aching and must empty their charge.
From her hooves to the horns that helplessly defend her, a rank scent
        surrounds her.

Comes to me thus, in the frieze at Lascaux,
Mother inconceivably disguised,
Wisdom, her eyes filled with tears.   [MH]

QUATRE FASCINANTS
* * *

IV

L'ALOUETTE

Extrême braise du ciel et première ardeur du jour,
Elle reste sertie dans l'aurore et chante la terre agitée,
Carillon maître de son haleine et libre de sa route.

Fascinante, on la tue en l'émerveillant.

LE REMPART DE BRINDILLES
* * *

VERS L'ARBRE-FRÈRE AUX JOURS COMPTÉS

Harpe brève des mélèzes,
Sur l'éperon de mousse et de dalles en germe
—Façade des forêts où casse le nuage—,
Contrepoint du vide auquel je crois.

FOUR FASCINATORS
* * *

IV

THE LARK

Sky's extreme ember, day's first flush,
She is forever set in dawn, singing the troubled earth,
A bell master of her breath and free in her ways,

She who fascinates, is dazzled to death.   [MAC]

THE RAMPART OF TWIGS
* * *

TO FRIEND-TREE OF COUNTED DAYS

Brief harp of the larches
On mossy spur of stone crop
—Façade of the forest,
Against which mists are shattered—
Counterpoint of the void in which
I believe.   [WCW]

L'INOFFENSIF

Je pleure quand le soleil se couche parce qu'il te dérobe à ma vue et parce que je ne sais pas m'accorder avec ses rivaux nocturnes. Bien qu'il soit au bas et maintenant sans fièvre, impossible d'aller contre son déclin, de suspendre son effeuillaison, d'arracher quelque envie encore à sa lueur moribonde. Son départ te fond dans son obscurité comme le limon du lit se délaye dans l'eau du torrent par-delà l'éboulis des berges détruites. Dureté et mollesse au ressort différent ont alors des effets semblables. Je cesse de recevoir l'hymne de ta parole; soudain tu n'apparais plus entière à mon côté; ce n'est pas le fuseau nerveux de ton poignet que tient ma main mais la branche creuse d'un quelconque arbre mort et déjà débité. On ne met plus un nom à rien, qu'au frisson. Il fait nuit. Les artifices qui s'allument me trouvent aveugle.

Je n'ai pleuré en vérité qu'une seule fois. Le soleil en disparaissant avait coupé ton visage. Ta tête avait roulé dans la fosse du ciel et je ne croyais plus au lendemain.

Lequel est l'homme du matin et lequel celui des ténèbres?

LE MORTEL PARTENAIRE

à Maurice Blanchot

Il la défiait, s'avançait vers son coeur, comme un boxeur ourlé, ailé et puissant, bien au centre de la géométrie attaquante et défensive de ses jambes. Il pesait du regard les qualités de l'adversaire qui se contentait de rompre, cantonné entre une virginité agréable et son expérience. Sur la blanche surface où se tenait le combat, tous deux oubliaient les spectateurs inexorables. Dans l'air de juin voltigeait le prénom des fleurs du premier jour de l'été. Enfin une légère grimace courut sur la joue du second et une raie rose s'y dessina. La riposte jaillit sèche et conséquente. Les jarrets soudain comme du linge étendu, l'homme flotta et tituba. Mais les poings en face ne poursuivirent pas leur avantage, renoncèrent à conclure. À présent les têtes meurtries des deux battants dodelinaient l'une contre l'autre. À cet instant le premier dut à dessein prononcer à l'oreille du second des paroles si parfaite-

THE HARMLESS MAN

I weep when the sun goes down because it takes you from my sight and I am not congenial with its nocturnal rivals. Although it is now low, and has no fever, I cannot keep it from declining, suspend its shedding of leaves, or glean more longing from its moribund glimmer. Going, it melts you in darkness, as the alluvium of the bed liquifies in the water of the current, out beyond the falling earth of the wasting banks. Hardness and softness differ in their origins, but here have similar effects. I am no longer granted the hymn of your words; suddenly you appear no longer whole at my side; this is not the nervous spindle of your wrist I hold in my hand but the hollow branch of some tree or other, dead and already sawed up. Nothing any longer has a name, except the shudder. It is night. The fireworks flaring show that I am blind.

I wept in truth only once. The sun when it disappeared cut off your face. Your head rolled into the grave of the sky and I no longer believed in tomorrow.

Which is the man for morning, and which for the dark?   [MAC]

THE MORTAL PARTNER

for Maurice Blanchot

He challenged her, went straight for her heart, like a boxer—trim, winged, powerful—centered in the offensive and defensive geometry of his legs. His glance weighed the fine points of his adversary who was content to break off fighting, suspended between a pleasant virginity and knowledge of him. On the white surface where the combat was being held, both forgot the inexorable spectators. The given names of the flowers of summer's first day fluttered in the June air. Finally a slight grimace crossed the adversary's cheek and a streak of pink appeared. The riposte flashed back, brusque and to the point. His legs suddenly like linen on the line, the man floated, staggered. But the opposing fists did not pursue their advantage, refusing to conclude the match. Now the two fighters' battered heads nodded against each other. At that instant the first must have purposely pronounced into the

ment offensantes, ou appropriées, ou énigmatiques, que de celui-ci fila, prompte, totale, précise, une foudre qui coucha net l'incompréhensible combattant.

Certains êtres ont une signification qui nous manque. Qui sont-ils? Leur secret tient au plus profond du secret même de la vie. Ils s'en approchent. Elle les tue. Mais l'avenir qu'ils ont ainsi éveillé d'un murmure, les devinant, les crée. Ô dédale de l'extrême amour!

VERMILLON

Réponse à un peintre.

Qu'elle vienne, maîtresse, à ta marche inclinée,
Ou qu'elle appelle de la brume du bois;
Qu'en sa chambre elle soit prévenue et suivie,
Épouse à son carreau, fusée inaperçue;
Sa main, fendant la mer et caressant tes doigts,
Déplace de l'été la borne invariable.

La tempête et la nuit font chanter, je l'entends,
Dans le fer de tes murs le galet d'Agrigente.

Fontainier, quel dépit de ne pouvoir tirer de son caveau mesquin
La source, notre endroit!

second's ear words so perfectly offensive, or appropriate, or enigmatic, that the latter let fly a lightning bolt, abrupt, complete, precise, which knocked the incomprehensible fighter out cold.

Certain beings have a meaning that escapes us. Who are they? Their secret resides in the deepest part of life's own secret. They draw near. Life kills them. But the future they have thus awoken with a murmur, sensing them, creates them. O labyrinth of utmost love!   [NK]

VERMILION

To a painter who questioned me.

Whether she comes, as mistress, to your beckoning stair,
Or whether she calls out of the wood haze;
Whether she be alert and followed in her chamber,
Wedded to her window, an unnoticed rocket;
Her hand, cleaving the sea and caressing your fingers,
Displaces the invariable bourn of summer.

I can hear night and the tempest making the beach-shingle
Of Agrigento sing in the iron of your walls.

Springmaker, what frustration to be unable to draw from its scanty hollow
The spring—the place that is our own!   [WSM]

MARMONNEMENT

Pour ne pas me rendre et pour m'y retrouver, je t'offense, mais combien je suis épris de toi, loup, qu'on dit à tort funèbre, pétri des secrets de mon arrière-pays. C'est dans une masse d'amour légendaire que tu laisses la déchaussure vierge, pourchassée de ton ongle. Loup, je t'appelle, mais tu n'as pas de réalité nommable. De plus, tu es inintelligible. Non-comparant, compensateur, que sais-je? Derrière ta course sans crinière, je saigne, je pleure, je m'enserre de terreur, j'oublie, je ris sous les arbres. Traque impitoyable où l'on s'acharne, où tout est mis en action contre la double proie: toi invisible et moi vivace.

Continue, va, nous durons ensemble; et ensemble, bien que séparés, nous bondissons par-dessus le frisson de la suprême déception pour briser la glace des eaux vives et se reconnaître là.

POUR RENOUER

Nous nous sommes soudain trop approchés de quelque chose dont on nous tenait à une distance mystérieusement favorable et mesurée. Depuis lors, c'est le rongement. Notre appuie-tête a disparu.

Il est insupportable de se sentir part solidaire et impuissante d'une beauté en train de mourir par la faute d'autrui. Solidaire dans sa poitrine et impuissant dans le mouvement de son esprit.

Si ce que je te montre et ce que je te donne te semblent moindres que ce que je te cache, ma balance est pauvre, ma glane est sans vertu.

Tu es reposoir d'obscurité sur ma face trop offerte, poème. Ma splendeur et ma souffrance se sont glissées entre les deux.

Jeter bas l'existence laidement accumulée et retrouver le regard qui l'aima assez à son début pour en étaler le fondement. Ce qui me reste à vivre est dans cet assaut, dans ce frisson.

MUMBLING

Not to surrender and so to take my bearings, I offend you, but how in love with you I am, wolf, wrongly called funereal, molded with the secrets of my back country. In a mass of legendary love you leave the trace, virgin, hunted, of your claw. Wolf, I call you, but you have no nameable reality. Moreover, you are unintelligible. By default, compensating, what else could I say? Behind your maneless running, I am bleeding, weeping; I gird myself with terror, I forget, I am laughing under the trees. Pitiless and unending pursuit, where all is set in motion against the double prey: you invisible and I perennial.

Go on, we endure together; and together, although separate, we bound over the tremor of supreme deception to shatter the ice of quick waters and recognize ourselves there.   [MAC]

TO RESUME

We suddenly got too close to something from which we'd been kept at a mysteriously favorable and measured distance. Since then, corrosion. Our headrest has disappeared.

It is unbearable to feel oneself a committed and impotent part of beauty that is dying through the fault of others. Committed in one's breast and impotent in the movement of one's mind.

If what I show you and what I give you seem less to you than what I hide, my weighing is poor, my reaping ineffectual.

You are, poem, a wayside altar of darkness on my too-exposed face. My splendor and my suffering have slipped between the two.

I must cast off life's ugly accumulation and find again the gaze that loved it enough in the beginning to display its foundation. What is left for me to live exists in this assault, this tremor.   [NK]

LE BOIS DE L'EPTE

Je n'étais ce jour-là que deux jambes qui marchent.
Aussi, le regard sec, le nul au centre du visage,
Je me mis à suivre le ruisseau du vallon.
Bas coureur, ce fade ermite ne s'immisçait pas
Dans l'informe où je m'étendais toujours plus avant.

Venus du mur d'angle d'une ruine laissée jadis par l'incendie,
Plongèrent soudain dans l'eau grise
Deux rosiers sauvages pleins d'une douce et inflexible volonté.
Il s'y devinait comme un commerce d'êtres disparus, à la veille de s'annoncer
    encore.

Le rauque incarnat d'une rose, en frappant l'eau,
Rétablit la face première du ciel avec l'ivresse des questions,
Éveilla au milieu des paroles amoureuses la terre,
Me poussa dans l'avenir comme un outil affamé et fiévreux.

Le bois de l'Epte commençait un tournant plus loin.
Mais je n'eus pas à le traverser, le cher grainetier du relèvement!
Je humai, sur le talon du demi-tour, le remugle des prairies où fondait une
    bête,
J'entendis glisser la peureuse couleuvre;
De chacun—ne me traitez pas durement—j'accomplissais, je le sus, les
    souhaits.

THE EPTE WOODS

I was nothing more that day than two legs walking.
My vision drained, a zero at the center of my face,
I took to following the stream that ran through the valley.
Low-lying, that dreary hermit had kept well clear
Of the formlessness into which I kept on pushing on.

From the cornerstone of a ruin formed once by fire,
Two wild rose-shrubs filled with great tenderness and determination
    emerged,
Plunging abruptly down into the gray water.
You could somehow sense the bustle of the departed, on the point of coming
    forward once more.

The harsh vermilions of a rose as it struck the water
In a rapture of questions restored the sky to its original aspect,
Rousing the earth to a chorus of loving tongues
And like a famished, feverish tool urging me on into the future.

At the next turning, the Epte woods began.
There would be no need to cross them, though, my beloved seed-sowers of
    recovery!
Half-turning, I breathed the damp must of the meadows where a beast was
    merging;
I heard the slither of the fearful grass-snake;
I did then—do not treat me harshly—what everyone, I knew, was hoping
    would be done.   [MH]

VICTOIRE ÉCLAIR

L'oiseau bêche la terre,
Le serpent sème,
La mort améliorée
Applaudit la récolte.

Pluton dans le ciel!

L'explosion en nous.
Là seulement dans moi.
Fol et sourd, comment pourrais-je l'être davantage?

Plus de second soi-même, de visage changeant, plus de saison pour la flamme
et de saison pour l'ombre!

Avec la lente neige descendent les lépreux.

Soudain l'amour, l'égal de la terreur,
D'une main jamais vue arrête l'incendie, redresse le soleil, reconstruit
l'Amie.

Rien n'annonçait une existence si forte.

LIGHTNING VICTORY

The bird tills the soil,
The serpent sows,
Death, enriched,
Praises the harvest.

Pluto in the sky!

In ourselves the explosion.
There in myself only.
Mad and deaf, how could I be more so?

No more second self, nor changing face, no more season of flame and season
    of shadow!

The lepers come down with the slow snow.

Suddenly love, the equal of terror,
With a hand I had never seen, puts an end to the fire, straightens the sun,
    reshapes the beloved.

Nothing had heralded so strong an existence.   [WSM]

LA CHAMBRE DANS L'ESPACE

Tel le chant du ramier quand l'averse est prochaine—l'air se poudre de pluie, de soleil revenant—, je m'éveille lavé, je fonds en m'élevant; je vendange le ciel novice.

Allongé contre toi, je meus ta liberté. Je suis un bloc de terre qui réclame sa fleur.

Est-il gorge menuisée plus radieuse que la tienne? Demander c'est mourir!

L'aile de ton soupir met un duvet aux feuilles. Le trait de mon amour ferme ton fruit, le boit.

Je suis dans la grâce de ton visage que mes ténèbres couvrent de joie.

Comme il est beau ton cri qui me donne ton silence!

INVITATION

J'appelle les amours qui roués et suivis par la faulx de l'été, au soir embaument l'air de leur blanche inaction.

Il n'y a plus de cauchemar, douce insomnie perpétuelle. Il n'y a plus d'aversion. Que la pause d'un bal dont l'entrée est partout dans les nuées du ciel.

Je viens avant la rumeur des fontaines, au final du tailleur de pierre.

Sur ma lyre mille ans pèsent moins qu'un mort.

J'appelle les amants.

THE ROOM IN SPACE

Such is the wood-pigeon's song when the shower approaches—the air is
   powdered with rain, with ghostly sunlight—
I awake washed, I melt as I rise, I gather the tender sky.

Lying beside you, I move your liberty.
I am a block of earth reclaiming its flower.

Is there a carved throat more radiant than yours? To ask is to die!

The wing of your sigh spreads a film of down on the leaves. The arrow of my
   love closes your fruit, drinks it.

I am in the grace of your countenance which my darkness covers with joy.

How beautiful your cry that gives me your silence!   [WSM]

INVITATION

   I summon the loves that, racked and followed by summer's scythe,
embalm the evening air with their white inactivity.

   No longer nightmare, soft perpetual sleeplessness. No more aversion.
Only the pause in a dance whose entrance is everywhere among the sky-
drifts.

   I come before the murmur of fountains, at the stonecutter's finale.

   On my lyre a thousand years weigh less than a dead man.

   I summon the lovers.   [MAC]

97

POURQUOI LA JOURNÉE VOLE

Le poète s'appuie, durant le temps de sa vie, à quelque arbre, ou mer, ou talus, ou nuage d'une certaine teinte, un moment, si la circonstance le veut. Il n'est pas soudé à l'égarement d'autrui. Son amour, son saisir, son bonheur ont leur equivalent dans tous les lieux où il n'est pas allé, où jamais il n'ira, chez les étrangers qu'il ne connaîtra pas. Lorsqu'on élève la voix devant lui, qu'on le presse d'accepter des égards qui retiennent, si l'on invoque à son propos les astres, il répond qu'il est du pays d'*à côté,* du ciel qui vient d'être englouti. Le poète vivifie puis court au dénouement.

Au soir, malgré sur sa joue plusieurs fossettes d'apprenti, c'est un passant courtois qui brusque les adieux pour être là quand le pain sort du four.

LE DEUIL DES NÉVONS

Pour un violon, une flûte et un écho.

Un pas de jeune fille
A caressé l'allée,
A traversé la grille.

Dans le parc des Névons
Les sauterelles dorment.
Gelée blanche et grêlons
Introduisent l'automne.

C'est le vent qui décide
Si les feuilles seront
À terre avant les nids.

＊

WHY THE DAY FLIES

During his lifetime the poet leans against some tree or sea or slope or cloud of a certain color, for a moment, if circumstance permits. He is not welded to other people's aberrations. His love, his captivation, his happiness have equivalents in all the places he has never been, will never go, in strangers he will never meet. When voices are raised before him, offering honors which would bind, if someone speaking of him invokes the stars, he answers that he's from the *next* country, from the sky just now engulfed.

The poet quickens, then races to the outcome.

In the evening, though dimpled like an apprentice, he is a courteous passerby who cuts his farewells short to be there when the bread comes out of the oven.　　　　　　　　　　　　　　　　　　　　　　　　　　　　　　[NK]

MOURNING AT NEVONS

For a violin, a flute and an echo.

The stride of a girl
Has caressed the lane,
Has passed through the gate.

In the park at Nevons
The grasshoppers sleep.
White frost and hailstones
Introduce autumn.

And the wind decides
Whether leaves will fall
Or the nests first.

*

Vite! Le souvenir néglige
Qui lui posa ce front,
Ce large coup d'oeil, cette verse,
Balancement de méduse
Au-dessus du temps profond.

Il est l'égal des verveines,
Chaque été coupées ras,
Le temps où la terre sème.

*

La fenêtre et le parc,
Le platane et le toit
Lançaient charges d'abeilles,
Du pollen au rayon,
De l'essaim à la fleur.

Un libre oiseau voilier,
Planant pour se nourrir,
Proférait des paroles
Comme un hardi marin.

Quand le lit se fermait
Sur tout mon corps fourbu,
De beaux yeux s'en allaient
De l'ouvrage vers moi.

L'aiguille scintillait;
Et je sentais le fil
Dans le trésor des doigts
Qui brodaient la batiste.

Quickly! Memory ignores
Who showed him this face,
This wide stare, this spillage,
This swaying as of a jellyfish
Above deep time.

It is like the vervain
Each summer cut to the ground,
The season of earth's seeding.

*

The window and the park,
The plane tree and the roof
Discharged loads of bees,
From pollen to honeycomb
From the swarm to the flower.

A free gliding bird
Hovering for his food
Flung down words
Like a hearty sailor.

When the bed closed
On my whole wearied body,
Fair eyes turned
From their work to me.

The needle glittered;
And I felt the thread
In the treasure of fingers
That edged the batiste.

Ah! lointain est cet âge.
Que d'années à grandir,
Sans père pour mon bras!

Tous ses dons répandus,
La rivière chérie
Subvenait aux besoins.
Peupliers et guitares
Ressuscitaient au soir
Pour fêter ce prodige
Où le ciel n'avait part.

Un faucheur de prairie
S'élevant, se voûtant,
Piquait les hirondelles,
Sans fin silencieux.

Sa quille retenue
Au limon de l'îlot,
Une barque était morte.

L'heure entre classe et nuit,
La ronce les serrant,
Des garnements confus
Couraient, cruels et sourds.
La brume les sautait,
De glace et maternelle.
Sur le bambou des jungles
Ils s'étaient modelés,
Chers roseaux voltigeants!

*

Le jardinier invalide sourit
Au souvenir de ses outils perdus,
Au bois mort qui se multiplie.

*

Ah! Far off is that time.
The years of growing,
And no father for my arm!

Spreading all her gifts,
The beloved stream
Came to my need.
Poplars and guitars
Revived at evening
To celebrate this marvel
In which heaven had no part.

A prairie reaper
Rising, bending,
Roused the swallows,
Endlessly silent.

Its keel stuck
In the slime of the islet,
A boat lay dead.

The hour between school and night,
The bramble gripping them,
A mixture of rascals
Ran, cruel and deaf.
The mist veered over them,
Icy and maternal.
On the bamboo of the jungles
They had been modeled,
Dear bobbing reeds!

*

The invalid gardener smiles
At the thought of the lost tools,
Of the dead wood multiplying.

*

Le bien qu'on se partage,
Volonté d'un défunt,
A broyé et détruit
La pelouse et les arbres,
La paresse endormie,
L'espace ténébreux
De mon parc des Névons.

Puisqu'il faut renoncer
À ce qu'on ne peut retenir,
Qui devient autre chose
Contre ou avec le cœur,—
L'oublier rondement,

Puis battre les buissons
Pour chercher sans trouver
Ce qui doit nous guérir
De nos maux inconnus
Que nous portons partout.

The estate divided
By the will of a dead man,
Has crushed and destroyed
The lawn and the trees,
The sleeping idleness,
The shadowy space
Of my park at Nevons.

Since one must give up
What one cannot keep,
Which becomes something else
Whether or no the heart wills—
Roundly forget it,

Then beat the bushes
To seek without finding
That which must cure us
Of the unknown ills
We bear with us everywhere.   [WSM]

DÉCLARER SON NOM

J'avais dix ans. La Sorgue m'enchâssait. Le soleil chantait les heures sur le sage cadran des eaux. L'insouciance et la douleur avaient scellé le coq de fer sur le toit des maisons et se supportaient ensemble. Mais quelle roue dans le cœur de l'enfant aux aguets tournait plus fort, tournait plus vite que celle du moulin dans son incendie blanc?

TRAVERSE

La colline qu'il a bien servie descend en torrent dans son dos. Les langues pauvres le saluent; les mulets au pré lui font fête. La face rose de l'ornière tourne deux fois vers lui l'onde de son miroir. La méchanceté dort. Il est tel qu'il se rêvait.

L'ALLÉGRESSE

Les nuages sont dans les rivières, les torrents parcourent le ciel. Sans saisie les journées montent en graine, meurent en herbe. Le temps de la famine et celui de la moisson, l'un sous l'autre dans l'air haillonneux, ont effacé leur différence. Ils filent ensemble, ils bivaquent! Comment la peur serait-elle distincte de l'espoir, passant raviné? Il n'y a plus de seuil aux maisons, de fumée aux clairières. Est tombé au gouffre le désir de chaleur—et ce peu d'obscurité dans notre dos où s'inquiétait la primevère dès qu'épiait l'avenir.

Pont sur la route des invasions, mentant au vainqueur, exorable au défait. Saurons-nous, sous le pied de la mort, si le cœur, ce gerbeur, ne doit pas précéder mais suivre?

ANNOUNCING ONE'S NAME

I was ten. The Sorgue enshrined me. The sun sang the hours upon the wise dial of the waters. Both sorrow and insouciance had sealed the weathercock onto the roof of the houses where, together, they stood propped. What wheel, though, in the heart of a watchful child turns swifter, more powerfully, than that of the mill with its white fire?   [GS]

SHORTCUT

The hill he has served so well descends torrential at his back. Poor tongues salute him; the mules in the meadow welcome him. The gulley's rose-hued face turns toward him twice the waters of its mirror. Meanness sleeps. He is as he dreamt himself to be.   [MAC]

JOYOUS

Clouds are in the rivers, torrents course through the sky. Unpicked, the days run to seed, perish in the green. The time of famine and the time of harvest, one beneath the other in the tattered air, have wiped out their difference. They slip by together, they encamp! How should fear be distinct from hope, furrowed passerby? No more threshold to the houses, nor smoke to the clearings. Fallen to the pit, the desire for warmth, and this slight darkness at our back where the primrose became restless at the future's peeping.

Bridge on the invader's path, deceptive to the victor, merciful to the undone. Shall we know, under the heel of death, if the heart, binder of sheaves, should not precede but follow?   [MAC]

L'ÉTERNITÉ À LOURMARIN

Albert Camus

Il n'y a plus de ligne droite ni de route éclairée avec un être qui nous a quittés. Où s'étourdit notre affection? Cerne après cerne, s'il approche c'est pour aussitôt s'enfouir. Son visage parfois vient s'appliquer contre le nôtre, ne produisant qu'un éclair glacé. Le jour qui allongeait le bonheur entre lui et nous n'est nulle part. Toutes les parties—presque excessives—d'une présence se sont d'un coup disloquées. Routine de notre vigilance. . . . Pourtant cet être supprimé se tient dans quelque chose de rigide, de désert, d'essentiel en nous, où nos millénaires ensemble font juste l'épaisseur d'une paupière tirée.

Avec celui que nous aimons, nous avons cessé de parler, et ce n'est pas le silence. Qu'en est-il alors? Nous savons, ou croyons savoir. Mais seulement quant le passé qui signifie s'ouvre pour lui livrer passage. Le voici à notre hauteur, puis loin, devant.

À l'heure de nouveau contenue où nous questionnons tout le poids d'énigme, soudain commence la douleur, celle de compagnon à compagnon, que l'archer, cette fois, ne transperce pas.

Nakedness Lost

THE POPLAR TREE'S EFFACEMENT

The hurricane is stripping the woods.
I lull the tender-eyed lightning to sleep.
Let the great wind where I tremble
Marry the earth where I grow.

Its breath sharpens my vigil.
How turbid it is, the hollow
Of the sullied streambed's lure!

A key will be my dwelling,
The feint of a fire the heart confirms;
And the air whose talon held it.   {NK}

CHERISHING THOUZON

When sorrow had hoisted him up onto its coveted rooftop, a simple evidence, mistlessly, came clear. He was no longer free as two oars in the middle of an ocean. The spellbinding desire of speech had, along with the black waters, subsided. He followed the diminished wake of the slight tremblings that, here and there, still persisted. Half-masked, a granite dove measured with its wings the scattered remains of the great, engulfed work. Upon the damp slopes, the trail of foam and the indigent course of broken forms. In the stringent era that had just opened, the right to harvest without the use of poisons would be outlawed. The rush of all the free and raving streams of creation had completely ceased. At the end of his life he would have to yield to the new audacity everything that immense patience, with each dawn, had granted him. The day whirled about Thouzon. Unlike the lichen, death hasn't effaced all hope of snow. In the hollow of the immersed town, the moon's horn was mixing the last blood with the first clay. {GS}

VENASQUE

Les gels en meute vous rassemblent,
Hommes plus ardents que buisson;
Les longs vents d'hiver vous vont pendre.
Le toit de pierre est l'échafaud
D'une église glacée debout.

LES PARAGES D'ALSACE

Je t'ai montré La Petite-Pierre, la dot de sa forêt, le ciel qui naît aux
    branches,
L'ampleur de ses oiseaux chasseurs d'autres oiseaux,
Le pollen deux fois vivant sous la flambée des fleurs,
Une tour qu'on hisse au loin comme la toile du corsaire,
Le lac redevenu le berceau du moulin, le sommeil d'un enfant.

Là où m'oppressa ma ceinture de neige,
Sous l'auvent d'un rocher moucheté de corbeaux,
J'ai laissé le besoin d'hiver.
Nous nous aimons aujourd'hui sans au-delà et sans lignée,
Ardents ou effacés, différents mais ensemble,
Nous détournant des étoiles dont la nature est de voler sans parvenir.

Le navire fait route vers la haute mer végétale.
Tous feux éteints il nous prend à son bord.
Nous étions levés dès avant l'aube dans sa mémoire.
Il abrita nos enfances, lesta notre âge d'or,
L'appelé, l'hôte itinérant, tant que nous croyons à sa vérité.

114

VENASQUE

The frosts round up the pack of you,
Men who burn hotter than any bush;
Winter's long winds mean to hang you.
The stone roof is the scaffold
Of a church frozen standing.   [JG]

THE LATITUDES OF ALSACE

I have shown you La Petite-Pierre, the dowry its forest provides and the sky
    being born in its branches.
The expanse of birds there that prey on other birds,
A pollen come twice to life under the blazing of flowers,
A tower hoisted on the horizon like a pirate's sail,
The lake once more a cradle for the mill and, for the infant, sleep.

There where my belt of snow was wearying me,
Under the lintel of a rock stippled with crows,
I have left the need for winter.
Today we love one another with neither lineage nor the life to come,
Ardent or retiring, different but together,
Turning from the stars whose nature it is to fly without attaining.

The vessel is on course for the vegetal high seas.
All lights extinguished, it takes us on board.
We had been up since before dawn in its memory.
It sheltered our childhood years, ballasted our golden age,
The called for, the traveling host for as long as we uphold its truth.

[MH]

115

DANSONS AUX BARONNIES

En robe d'olivier   l'Amoureuse
  avait dit:
          Croyez à ma très enfantine fidélité.
       Et depuis,
  une vallée ouverte
              une côte qui brille
  un sentier d'alliance
        ont envahi la ville
  où la libre douleur est sous le vif de l'eau.

YVONNE

La Soif hospitalière
Qui l'entendit jamais se plaindre?

Nulle autre qu'elle n'aurait pu boire sans mourir les quarante fatigues,
Attendre, loin devant, ceux qui viendront après;
De l'éveil au couchant sa manœuvre était mâle.

Qui a creusé le puits et hisse l'eau gisante
Risque son cœur dans l'écart de ses mains.

LET'S GO DANCE AT LES BARONNIES

In olive-tree dress
                    the Girl in Love
          had said:
                    Trust my truly childlike faithfulness.
                    And since then,
     an open valley
                    a gleaming coast
     a path of assent
                    have invaded the town
     where free pain is under the quick of the water   [JG]

YVONNE

Bountiful Thirst

Who ever heard her complain?

None other but she could have drunk forty trials and not perished,
Nor awaited, far ahead, those coming after,
From waking to setting her way was a man's.

Whoever has dug the well and raised the sleeping water
Risks her heart in the hollow of her hands.   [MAC]

LIED DU FIGUIER

Tant il gela que les branches laiteuses
Molestèrent la scie, se cassèrent aux mains.
Le printemps ne vit pas verdir les gracieuses.

Le figuier demanda au maître du gisant
L'arbuste d'une foi nouvelle.
Mais le loriot, son prophète,
L'aube chaude de son retour,
En se posant sur le désastre,
Au lieu de faim, périt d'amour.

LENTEUR DE L'AVENIR

Il faut escalader beaucoup de dogmes et de glace pour jouer de bonheur et s'éveiller rougeur sur la pierre du lit.

Entre eux et moi il y eut longtemps comme une haie sauvage dont il nous était loisible de recueillir les aubépines en fleurs, et de nous les offrir. Jamais plus loin que la main et le bras. Ils m'aimaient et je les aimais. Cet obstacle *pour le vent* où échouait ma pleine force, quel était-il? Un rossignol me le révéla, et puis une charogne.

La mort dans la vie, c'est inalliable, c'est répugnant; la mort avec la mort, c'est approchable, ce n'est rien, un ventre peureux y rampe sans trembler.

J'ai renversé le dernier mur, celui qui ceinture les nomades des neiges, et je vois—ô mes premiers parents—l'été du chandelier.

Notre figure terrestre n'est que le second tiers d'une poursuite continue, un point, amont.

LIED OF THE FIG TREE

So much it froze that the milky branches
Hurt the saw, and snapped in the hands.
Spring didn't see the gracious ones turn green.

From the master of the felled, the fig tree
Asked for the shrub of a new faith.
But the oriole, its prophet,
The warm dawn of his return,
Alighting upon the disaster,
Instead of hunger, died of love.   [GS]

SLOWNESS OF THE FUTURE

One has to scale so much ice and dogma before attaining pleasure and awaking—flushed—on the stone of the bed.

For some time there'd been, between them and me, something like a wild hedge. We were free to pick and offer one another its flowering hawthorn. But never further than a hand's, an arm's length. They loved me just as I loved them. What was it, though, that obstacle *to the wind* in which my full strength failed? It was a nightingale that first revealed it to me, then carrion.

Death in life is repugnant, nonalloyable; death, however, within death is something accessible, is nothing: a frightened belly could crawl there without trembling.

I have overthrown the last wall, the one that encircles the snow nomads, and I see—o my very first parents—the candelabra's summer.

Our figure on earth is only the second third of a continuous pursuit, a point, upland.   [GS]

LUTTEURS

Dans le ciel des hommes, le pain des étoiles me sembla ténébreux et durci, mais dans leurs mains étroites je lus la joute de ces étoiles en invitant d'autres: émigrantes du pont encore rêveuses; j'en recueillis la sueur dorée, et par moi la terre cessa de mourir.

RÉMANENCE

De quoi souffres-tu? Comme si s'éveillait dans la maison sans bruit l'ascendant d'un visage qu'un aigre miroir semblait avoir figé. Comme si, la haute lampe et son éclat abaissés sur une assiette aveugle, tu soulevais vers ta gorge serrée la table ancienne avec ses fruits. Comme si tu revivais tes fugues dans la vapeur du matin à la rencontre de la révolte tant chérie, elle qui sut, mieux que toute tendresse, te secourir et t'élever. Comme si tu condamnais, tandis que ton amour dort, le portail souverain et le chemin qui y conduit.

De quoi souffres-tu?

De l'irréel intact dans le réel dévasté. De leurs détours aventureux cerclés d'appels et de sang. De ce qui fut choisi et ne fut pas touché, de la rive du bond au rivage gagné, du présent irréfléchi qui disparaît. D'une étoile qui s'est, la folle, rapprochée et qui va mourir avant moi.

WRESTLERS

In the sky of men, the star's bread seemed to me shadowy and hardened, but in their narrow hands I read the joust of these stars calling others: emigrants from below deck still dreaming; I gathered their golden sweat, and through me the earth ceased to die.   [MAC]

REMANENCE

From what do you suffer? As if in the noiseless house there were to awake the ascendancy of a face that an acrid mirror seemed to have fixed. As if, the high lamp and its radiance inclined over a blind plate, you were to lift toward your anguished throat the old table with its fruits. As if you were reliving your escapades in the morning haze toward the beloved revolt, which better than all tenderness, could succor you and raise you. As if condemning, while your love sleeps, the sovereign portal and the path leading toward it.

From what do you suffer?

From the unreal intact in reality laid waste. From their venturesome deviations circled with cries and blood. From that which was chosen and left untouched, from the shore of the leap to the coast attained, from the unreflecting present that disappears. From a star which, foolish, came close and will die before me.   [MAC]

La Nuit talismanique

VÉTÉRANCE

Maintenant que les apparences trompeuses, les miroirs piquetés se multiplient devant les yeux, nos traces passées deviennent véridiquement les sites où nous nous sommes agenouillés pour boire. Un temps immense, nous n'avons circulé et saigné que pour capter les traits d'une aventure commune. Voici que dans le vent brutal nos signes passagers trouvent, sous l'humus, la réalité de ces poudreuses enjambées qui lèvent un printemps derrière elles.

ÉPROUVANTE SIMPLICITÉ

Mon lit est un torrent aux plages desséchées. Nulle fougère n'y cherche sa patrie. Où t'es-tu glissé tendre amour?

Je suis parti pour longtemps. Je revins pour partir.

Plus loin, l'une des trois pierres du berceau de la source tarie disait ce seul mot gravé pour le passant: "Amie."

J'inventai un sommeil et je bus sa verdeur sous l'empire de l'été.

Talismanic Night

VETERANCE

Now that deceptive appearances, all the pockmarked mirrors, are multiplying before our eyes, our past traces truly become the sites where we have knelt to drink. For an immeasurable time we moved about and bled only to capture the features of a common adventure. And so in the brutal wind our passing signs find the reality, beneath the humus, of those powdery strides which stir up spring behind them. [NK]

A TRYING SIMPLICITY

My bed is a torrent with dried-up banks. No fern looks for its country there. Where have you hidden, my love?

I left for a long time. I came back to leave.

Farther on, one of three stones cradled in the exhausted spring spoke this single word engraved deeply for the passerby: "Friend."

I invented a sleep and drank its greenness under the sway of summer.

[MAC]

A Faulx contente

"QUAND LES CONSÉQUENCES . . ."

Quand les conséquences ne sont plus niées, le poème respire, dit qu'il a obtenu son aire. Iris rescapé de la crue des eaux.

Le souffle levé, descendre à reculons, puis obliquer et suivre le sentier qui ne mène qu'au cœur ensanglanté de soi, source et sépulcre du poème.

L'influx de milliards d'années de toutes parts et circulairement le chant jamais rendu d'Orphée.

Les dieux sont dans la métaphore. Happée par le brusque écart, la poésie s'augmente d'un au-delà sans tutelle.

Le poème nous couche dans une douleur ajournée sans séparer le froid de l'ardent.

Vint un soir où le cœur ne se reconnut plus dans les mots qu'il prononçait pour lui seul.

Le poète fait éclater les liens de ce qu'il touche. Il n'enseigne pas la fin des liens.

To Your Heart's Content

"THE CONSEQUENCES . . ."

The consequences no longer denied, the poem breathes, says it has not reached its own domain. Iris escaped from the rising of the waters.

High in breath, climb down backwards, then cut across and follow the path which only leads to the bloodied heart of the self, source and sepulcher of the poem.

Billions of years flowing in the influx from everywhere, and circular, the song of Orpheus, never at an end.

The gods are in metaphor. Snatched up in the sudden swerve, poetry gains a beyond without guardian.

The poem lays us down in pain adjourned without separating the cold from the ardent.

There came an evening when the heart no longer recognized itself in the words it pronounced for itself alone.
The poet bursts the bonds of what he touches. He does not teach the end of bonds. [MAC & PT]

Le Bâton de rosier

DE MOMENT EN MOMENT

Pourquoi ce chemin plutôt que cet autre? Où mène-t-il pour nous solliciter si fort? Quels arbres et quels amis sont vivants derrière l'horizon de ces pierres, dans le lointain miracle de la chaleur? Nous sommes venus jusqu'ici car là où nous étions ce n'était plus possible. On nous tourmentait et on allait nous asservir. Le monde, de nos jours, est hostile aux Transparents. Une fois de plus, il a fallu partir . . . Et ce chemin, qui ressemblait à un long squelette, nous a conduits à un pays qui n'avait que son souffle pour escalader l'avenir. Comment montrer, sans les trahir, les choses simples dessinées entre le crépuscule et le ciel? Par la vertu de la vie obstinée, dans la boucle du Temps artiste, entre la mort et la beauté.

1949.

The Rosebriar Stick

FROM MOMENT TO MOMENT

Why this road rather than that one? Calling us so urgently, where does it lead? What trees and friends are alive behind the horizon of these stones, in the distant miracle of heat? We have come this far because where we were, things were no longer possible. They were tormenting us. We would have been subservient. The world, these days, is hostile to the Transparents. Once more we had to leave . . . And this road, which looked like a long skeleton, led us to a country which could use only its own breath to climb the future. How can we show, without betraying them, those simple things sketched between the twilight and the sky? By the virtue of stubborn life, in the circle of artist Time, between death and beauty.   [MAC & PT]

1949.

Aromates chasseurs

ÉVADÉ D'ARCHIPEL

Orion,
Pigmenté d'infini et de soif terrestre,
N'épointant plus sa flèche à la faucille ancienne,
Les traits noircis par le fer calciné,
Le pied toujours prompt à éviter la faille,
Se plut avec nous
Et resta.

Chuchotement parmi les étoiles.

RÉCEPTION D'ORION

Qui cherchez-vous brunes abeilles
Dans la lavande qui s'éveille?
Passe votre roi serviteur.
Il est aveugle et s'éparpille.
Chasseur il fuit
Les fleurs qui le poursuivent.
Il tend son arc et chaque bête brille.
Haute est sa nuit; flèches risquez vos chances.

Un météore humain a la terre pour miel.

ÉBRIÉTÉ

Tandis que la moisson achevait de se graver sur le cuivre du soleil, une alouette chantait dans la faille du grand vent sa jeunesse qui allait prendre fin. L'aube d'automne parée de ses miroirs déchirés de coups de feu, dans trois mois retentirait.

Hunting Herbs

ESCAPED FROM THE ARCHIPELAGO

Orion,
Pigmented by infinity and earthly thirst,
No longer whetting his arrow on the ancient sickle,
His countenance darkened by the calcinated iron,
His foot always ready to avoid the fault,
Was content in our midst
And remained.

Whispering among the stars.   [MAC]

ORION'S RECEPTION

Dark bees, whom are you seeking
In the lavender awaking?
Your servant king is passing by.
Blind, he strays, dispersing.
A hunter, he flees
The flowers pursuing him.
He bends his bow, each creature shines.
High is his night; arrows take your chance.

A human meteor has the earth for honey.   [MAC]

INEBRIATION

While the harvest finished etching itself on the sun's copper, a lark sang in
a fault of the great wind its youth which was to end. Autumn's dawn,
bejeweled with mirrors torn by gunshot, in three months would resound.

[NK]

Chants de la Balandrane

VERRINE

Le printemps prétendant porte des verres bleus et, de haut, regarde l'hiver aux yeux terre de Sienne. Se lever matin pour les surprendre ensemble! Je rends compte ici de ma fraîche surprise. Trois villages dans la brume au premier pli du jour. Le Ventoux ne tarderait pas à écarter le soleil du berceau gigantesque où trois de ses enfants dormaient emmaillotés de tuiles; soleil qui l'avait désigné souverain en s'élevant à l'est, riverain en le baignant encore avant de disparaître. Au clocher de l'église fourbue, l'heure enfonçait son clou, valet dont nul ne voulait plus.

LE BRUIT DE L'ALLUMETTE

J'ai été élevé parmi les feux de bois, au bord de braises qui ne finissaient pas cendres. Dans mon dos l'horizon tournant d'une vitre safranée réconciliait le plumet brun des roseaux avec le marais placide. L'hiver favorisait mon sort. Les bûches tombaient sur cet ordre fragile maintenu en suspens par l'alliance de l'absurde et de l'amour. Tantôt m'était soufflé au visage l'embrasement, tantôt une âcre fumée. Le héros malade me souriait de son lit lorsqu'il ne tenait pas clos ses yeux pour souffrir. Auprès de lui, ai-je appris à rester silencieux? À ne pas barrer la route à la chaleur grise? À confier le bois de mon cœur à la flamme qui le conduirait à des étincelles ignorées des enclaves de l'avenir? Les dates sont effacées et je ne connais pas les convulsions du compromis.

*

N'ayant que le souffle, je me dis qu'il sera aussi malaisé et incertain de se retrouver plus tard au coin d'un feu de bois parmi les étincelles, qu'en cette nuit de gelée blanche, sur un sentier ossu d'étoiles infortunées.

Songs of the Balandrane

VERRINE

Through sky-blue spectacles, aspiring Spring looks down on winter with the dark sienna eyes. Rise early and you will find them together. A word then while the gift is fresh. The first of the day's folds held three villages in the mist. Before long, though, the Ventoux had brushed the sun back from the gigantic cradle where three of his children lay sleeping, swaddled with tiles; a sun that would name the cradle sovereign by rising in the East, then riverrun by bathing it in light once more before departing. In the belfry of the ruined church, the hour drove the nail home, a valet whom no one had time for anymore.   [MH]

THE CRACKLING OF THE MATCH

I was raised amongst wood fires, next to embers which did not end in ashes. At my back the shifting horizon of the saffron window brought together the reed's dusky plume with the quiet marsh. Winter was kind to my fate. The logs were falling on this fragile order held suspended by the alliance of love and the absurd. Now the burning would blow on my face, now an acrid smoke. The sick hero smiled at me from his bed when he did not close his eyes, to suffer. Did I learn silence by his side? Not to bar the way to the ashen heat? To give over the wood of my heart to the flame which would reduce it to sparks unknown in the recesses of the future? The dates have been erased and the convulsions of compromise are not mine.

*

Having only my breath, I tell myself that one would be just as uneasy and uncertain to find oneself later beside a wood fire amongst the sparks, as in this night of whited frost, upon a path studded with ill-fated stars.   [MAC & CP]

Fenêtres dormantes et porte sur le toit

LÉGÈRETÉ DE LA TERRE

Le repos, la planche de vivre? Nous tombons. Je vous écris en cours de chute. C'est ainsi que j'éprouve l'état d'être au monde. L'homme se défait aussi sûrement qu'il fut jadis composé. La roue du destin tourne à l'envers et ses dents nous déchiquettent. Nous prendrons feu bientôt du fait de l'accélération de la chute. L'amour, ce frein sublime, est rompu, hors d'usage.

Rien de cela n'est écrit sur le ciel assigné, ni dans le livre convoité qui se hâte au rythme des battements de notre cœur, puis se brise alors que notre cœur continue à battre.

LE DOIGT MAJEUR

Au terme du tourbillon des marches, la porte n'a pas de verrou de sûreté: c'est le toit. Je suis pour ma joie au cœur de cette chose, ma douleur n'a plus d'emploi. Comme dans les travaux d'aiguille, cette disposition n'a qu'un point de retenue: de la pierre à soleil à l'ardoise bleuâtre. Il suffirait que le doigt majeur se séparât de la main et, à la première mousse entre deux tuiles glissantes, innocemment le passage s'ouvrirait.

RÉCIT ÉCOURTÉ

Tout ce qui illuminait à l'intérieur de nous gisait maintenant à nos pieds. Hors d'usage. L'intelligence que nous recevons du monde matériel, avec les multiples formes au-dehors nous comblant de bienfaits, se détournait de nos besoins. Le miroir avait brisé tous ses sujets. On ne frète pas le vent ni ne descend le cours de la tempête. Ne grandit pas la peur, n'augmente pas le courage. Nous allons derechef répéter le projet suivant, jusqu'à la réalité du retour qui délivrera un nouveau départ de concert. Enserre de ta main le poignet de la main qui te tend le plus énigmatique des cadeaux: une riante flamme levée, éprise de sa souche au point de s'en séparer.

Dormer Windows and Door on the Roof

EARTH'S PRECARIOUSNESS

Rest at last, then, the life raft? We fall. I write to you in the midst of my descent. It is thus that I feel the state of being at one with the world. Mankind is coming apart as surely as it was once composed. The wheel of destiny is running backwards and its teeth are tearing us apart. Our rate of acceleration is such that we will soon catch fire. Love, that sublime brake, is broken, no longer serviceable.

None of this is written on the assigned sky, nor in the longed-for book that hurries forward to the rhythm of our heartbeats, then shatters while our heart continues beating.   [MH]

MIDDLE FINGER

At the top of the swirling stairs, the door has no safety bolt: it's the roof. I am to my joy at the heart of this thing, my suffering no longer serves. As in needlework, this frame of mind has only one stitch to hold it: from the stone of the sun to the bluish slate. It would be enough for the middle finger to separate from the hand and, at the first moss between two slippery tiles, innocently the passage would open.   [NK]

A TALE CUT SHORT

Everything that illuminated us within lay now at our feet. Beyond repair. The intelligence we get from the material world, its multiple outside forms filling us with blessings, turned away from our needs. The mirror had broken all its subjects. We do not charter the wind nor descend the wake of the storm. Fear does not grow, courage does not augment. We are yet again going to rehearse the next scheme, till the return that offers a new concerted departure becomes reality. With your hand take the wrist of the hand that holds out to you the most enigmatic of gifts: a laughing lifted flame, enough in love with its stalk to leave it.   [NK]

ÉPRISE

Chaque carreau de la fenêtre est un morceau de mur en face, chaque pierre scellée du mur une recluse bienheureuse qui nous éclaire matin, soir, de poudre d'or à ses sables mélangée. Notre logis va son histoire. Le vent aime à y tailler.

L'étroit espace où se volatilise cette fortune est une petite rue au-dessous dont nous n'apercevons pas le pavé. Qui y passe emporte ce qu'il désire.

IN LOVE

Each windowpane is a part of the facing wall, each stone sealed in the wall a blessed recluse lighting our morning, our evening with the gold dust mixed into its sands. Our dwelling lives out its fate. The wind loves to cut into it.

The narrow space where this fortune spins away is a little street below, whose paving we cannot see. Whoever passes there takes from it what he wishes. [MAC & PT]

Les Voisinages de Van Gogh

LA LONGUE PARTANCE

Avec le docile reflet de sa silhouette d'un boxeur sur l'eau, je me suis endormi. Ensuite j'ai oublié l'essentiel des restes de ma vie là-bas, là-bas, magnétisant encore.

Je n'avais pas emporté la ligne étroite de mon retour. J'avais l'approbation de mes matins et celle d'un ruisseau piétiné.

Les prévoyants, les offensés demeurent loin des chicanes du pouvoir. L'avenir aurait une parole pour eux qui les rapprocherait solitairement du soleil et de ses conventions, et plus tard d'une ombre sans anneau. Je me souciais peu de trouver des traces plus anciennes. Bien que l'âge se fût emparé d'elles, les formes les plus fines dessinaient sur la nue des lopins remuants.

C'est ainsi que je rencontrai un homme non las, s'étoilant de privations. J'eus grande envie de m'éloigner, mais sans vaciller je courus à ses côtés, vers plus évident!

La vaste mer, il me semble, sans tempête et sans chaleur.

SOCIÉTÉ

Nous étions en décembre, la nuit s'habillait tôt. Une fougueuse pluie s'emmêlait dans un vent glaçant et lui portait des coups de pointe. Quelques chasseurs se dissimulaient dans un taillis, un genou sur les brindilles. Leur gibier migrateur par ce temps maudit était un vol de grives apeurées; l'œil des tireurs, sur leurs riches terres aux plants trop bien alignés, imaginait les oiseaux au couchant, pressés de mourir.

Les fonds de lit sont zélés mais très froids.

In the Vicinity of Van Gogh

LONG IN LEAVING

With the reflection of a boxer's profile submissive on the waters, I fell asleep. Then I forgot the essential in what remained of my life beyond, beyond, still attracting.

I had not taken with me the thin line of my return. I had the approval of my mornings and that of a trampled stream.

The farsighted, the insulted, dwell far off from the dealings of power. The future may, with a word, bring them one by one nearer to the sun and its rituals, and later, to a shadow unringed.
I cared little about finding former traces. Although age had gripped them, the most delicate forms sketched upon the skies a few quavering shreds.

So it is that I met a man not yet weary, resplendent with privations. I longed to take my distance, but unhesitating I ran beside him, towards the clearing.

The vast sea, it seems to me, without storm or heat.   [MAC & CP]

SOCIETY

It was in December, when the nights dress early. An unruly rain had got itself entangled in an icy wind and was taking stabs at it. In a copse nearby, hunters were hiding, one knee poised on the twigs beneath them. Their migratory game in this dismal weather was a flight of panicking thrushes; the marksmen's eyes, on these rich lands of theirs where the plots were too neatly aligned, imagined the birds at sunset, in a hurry to die.
The depths of a bed are zealous but very cold.   [MH]

Éloge d'une Soupçonnée

LE REGARD À TERRE

Les pétales s'ouvrent et s'étendent, sortent de la ronde, escortés par la mort, adjoints un instant au cœur révoquant de la rose.

La rose, l'équivalente d'une vaillante étoile qu'un parfum plus distant aurait touché, lui donnant la couleur d'un astre non commun.

Et la voici informe demandant aux éclairs dans le ciel un peu de leur courroux . . . Terre, convoitise des maraudeurs, hier prompte à nous impliquer! La luisance bleutée vient de nous parvenir.

L'un d'entre eux a dit, l'index pointé: "C'est l'étoile des rats! La seule dont l'ombre me demeure limpide."

De controverse point! Mais du grief au malheur, à coup sûr.

Rose au nombre confondu où prédominaient vieillards et enfants, sur cette base incertaine la joute a pris fin. Effeuillaison de la rose. Dissipation de l'étoile.

SOUS UNE PLUIE DE PIERRES, LES OGRES . . .

Sous une pluie de pierres, nous nous en tiendrons à notre gisement soldé par le passé en émoi. Montant d'un avenir captieux, le présent au solide appétit, aux largesses imprévisibles, en restera à de passionnés desseins. Pas d'éploration.

In Praise of One Suspected

LOOKING AT THE EARTH

The petals open and extend, come out of the round, escorted by death, joined for a moment to the revoking heart of the rose.

The rose, the equivalent of a valiant star that a more distant scent would have touched, giving it the color of an uncommon orb.

And here it is, imperfect, asking of the flashes in the sky a little of their ire . . . Earth, marauders' covetousness, yesterday quick to implicate us! The blue-tinted brightness only now reaches us.

One of them said, pointing: "That's the star of the rats! The only one whose shadow stays clear to me."

No controversy! But some grievance at misfortune, assuredly.

Rose indistinguishable in number where old folk and children predominated, on this uncertain base has the contest ended. Shedding of the rose. Dissipation of the star.   [CC]

UNDER A STORM OF STONES, THE OGRES . . .

Under a storm of stones, we will be content with our lode paid for by past turmoils. Rising from a captious future, the present with its healthy appetite, its unpredictable bounty, will retain its passionate projects. No weeping . . .   [MAC & CP]

L'AMANTE

à M. C. C.

Tant la passion m'avait saisi pour cette amante délectable, moi non exempt d'épanchement et d'oscillante lubricité, je devais, ne devais pas mourir en sourdine ou modifié, reconnu des seules paupières de mon amante. Les nuits de nouveauté sauvage avaient retrouvé l'ardente salive communicante, et parfumé son appartenance fiévreuse. Mille précautions altérées me conviaient à la plus voluptueuse chair qui soit. À nos mains un désir d'outre destin, quelle crainte à nos lèvres demain?

THE LOVER

for M. C. C.

I'd been so seized by passion for this delectable lover. I not exactly exempt from feeling, from tremblors of lust. It meant I must, meant I absolutely must not, just fade away quietly, mildly changed, recognized only by the eyelids of my lover. Nights of savage newness found for me again the flaming saliva that connects and perfumed the fevered connection. A thousand precautions gave way thirstily to the most voluptuous flesh there could be. In our hands desire that transcends. What fear on our lips tomorrow?

[FS]

The editors would like to express their grateful appreciation to Marie-Claude Char, to Jerôme Lindon, literary executor of Samuel Beckett, and to James Laughlin and Peter Glassgold of New Directions.

Library of Congress Cataloging in Publication Data

Char, René, 1907–
    [Poems. Selections. English & French. 1992]
    Selected poems of René Char / edited by Mary Ann Caws and Tina
Jolas.
      p.   cm.
    English and French.
    Includes bibliographical references.
    ISBN 0–8112–1191–6. — ISBN 0–8112–1192–4 (pbk.)
    1. Char, René, 1907–   —Translations into English.   I. Caws,
Mary Ann.   II. Jolas, Tina.   III. Title.
PQ2605.H3345A23   1992
841'.912—dc20
                                   92–6351
                                    CIP